FENG
SHUI
LIFE PLANNER

LILLIAN TOO

FENG SHUI
LIFE PLANNER

hamlyn

First published in Great Britain in 2003 by

Hamlyn, a division of Octopus Publishing Group Ltd

2–4 Heron Quays, London E14 4JP

Distributed in the United States and Canada by

Sterling Publishing Co., Inc.

387 Park Avenue South, New York, NY 10016–8810

ISBN 0 600 60902 2

A CIP catalogue record for this book is available
from the British Library

Printed and bound in China

1 3 5 7 9 10 8 6 4 2

CONTENTS

INTRODUCTION

Translated literally, feng shui means 'wind water'. These two words in actual fact describe a precious living skill that has been known to and practised by the Chinese for several thousand years. Feng shui is the practice of creating a happy living environment within the home – one that is positive and beneficial at all times.

Good feng shui reflects the right balance of yin and yang energy while simultaneously ensuring there is harmony between the five elements – earth, fire, air, water and metal – that make up the cosmic universe we live in.

ABOVE The use of symbolism is an important part of feng shui. Certain images and objects, such as the water-spouting dragon, are imbued with magical powers that can bring you good luck and deter bad luck.

Good feng shui is created by arranging the flow of energy in one's environment in a way that attracts good fortune – health, wealth and happiness – to residents. There are a few basic principles to follow and these relate to space enhancement as well as time enhancement.

When practised correctly, the principles of feng shui can create exceptional good luck in all aspects of one's life – love, family, health, wealth and career. It can protect against misfortunes, sickness and loss of income.

Feng shui is based on the principle that life in the material world should be made as comfortable as possible and to do this one should live in harmony with the chi energy that encompasses your space, and that transforms with the passage of time.

This book is written as a very easy guide to enable you to do both – to live in harmony with the energy of your space as well as adapt to the changing cycles of chi patterns that take place over time. Both principles are addressed to enable you to be protected at all times against bad feng shui, and teach you how to create good feng shui. Using this book as a guide you can design your space and plan your life to flow positively in sync with the energy of your home. Feng shui can be used from a very young age to enhance your education luck, and when you are older you can use it to give your career luck a huge boost. Feng shui is also especially helpful for those of you who wish to attract a good relationship into your life and to help you build a meaningful professional/ business life – one that attracts material success. You can use it to create a nurturing environment for your family to enjoy health and prosperity. Indeed there are so many aspects to mankind's aspirations, and the complete practice of feng shui can bring good fortune to all of them.

Feng Shui Life Planner introduces you to your Kua number – the feng shui way of working out your personalized good and bad directions based on the Eight Mansions formula. This is such a wonderfully potent and easy-to-use method of feng shui that once you use it and feel its instant effect, it will forever influence the way you sit, how you sleep, work, and even how the doors and rooms you use are oriented. This method of feng shui is the easiest and arguably the most powerful of feng shui methods, which I introduced to the West in my first book on feng shui published in 1997.

Once you have mastered the Eight Mansions formula, you can move on to period cycles of feng shui, which incorporate the House Trigram formula and Flying Star methods. These address the time changes of energy within a home or work space. The method offers an accurate map of the luck of a household. Using this method you can identify the wealth spots in your home and the good relationship corners, as well as those parts of the home that are vulnerable to

ABOVE Feng shui will enable you to look at your living space differently. This living room looks pretty and appealing and the sunlight filtering in brings benevolent yang chi. However there are problems here, particularly in the sharp angles created by the dividing wall, which cause disruptive chi.

illness and misfortunes. The idea of having this luck map of your house – referred to in the book as the natal charts – is that you can then activate the wealth spots and auspicious relationship areas to ensure that particular luck is activated and maximized. You can place potent cures in areas of your home that are seriously afflicted by illness and misfortune chi energy.

You will be amazed by how quickly good luck manifests – often in ways you least expect!

Once you have grasped the principles of feng shui it is very easy to work with and you will find it becomes a natural part of your life. It may seem daunting at first, with so many guidelines to remember, so go slowly. Once you have made a few changes to your interior design and started to appreciate the harmony that emerges, you will be encouraged to persevere, and then feng shui becomes a valuable living skill. You will be pleasantly surprised by how fast you pick it all up and also how much of it seems familiar. This is because so much of feng shui is good old common sense.

BELOW The Laughing Buddha holding ingots and wearing red robes is a very lucky feng shui image. Feng shui is adaptable however, and an image of Santa Claus would be just as potent, since he too is shown smiling and wearing red.

Of course, harmonious living depends on not one but all the residents of the home. If there are four members in your family – two parents and two children – and your personal Kua numbers indicate that three of you should be sleeping in the bedroom in the southwest sector of the home, what do you do? The answer is to take advantage of feng shui's flexibility. Allocate bedrooms in the most appropriate way according to size and need, and then allow each person to personalize their space. The shared areas, such as the living and dining rooms and the kitchen, can be enhanced in ways that benefit the whole family.

Feng Shui Life Planner gives you all you need to practise feng shui successfully – there are clear explanations at every level of practice from the most basic to the more advanced formulas, and most of the relevant charts and tables have been simplified without losing any of their essence. Some of the charts in this book, for instance, successfully encapsulate even the thousand-year-old calendar of the Chinese into simple, user-friendly tables – indeed these charts represent some of the more valuable pages of this book. When you start using them is when you will start to love them!

In addition, of course, there are plenty of interior design ideas you can incorporate into your practice. When you have become good at feng shui, there is nothing to stop you from adapting the principles stated here to your particular culture or tradition.

The first part of *Feng Shui Life Planner* introduces the basic concepts of feng shui and explains the three formulas that enable you to work out personal charts for your home. The latter part of the book, beginning with Feng Shui in Action, shows you how to put what you have learnt about the 'luck' of your home into practice, with detailed advice on how you can attract good luck and repel bad luck room by room. The final chapter on Taoist feng shui shows you how to use symbols and interpret mystical signs to enhance your feng shui practise.

Throughout the book I use tables and charts to help explain the formulas. I also use example houses to illustrate how to apply the formulas to different shaped and oriented houses and rooms, so that you will be able to apply the fascinating science of feng shui to your own home.

Since each section builds upon knowledge from the previous section, it is best to work through the book from front to back, expanding your knowledge and expertise as you read.

LEFT Feng shui offers you advice about what to place where in a room to bring you, as an individual, good luck. So, for example, though flowers are beneficial to all people, they are particularly helpful to some.

UNDERSTANDING FENG SHUI

For those of you who are completely new to feng shui, or for those who have a vague knowledge that needs consolidating, this chapter covers the few basic essential concepts that are fundamental to its practice, from the concept of chi, which underpins the whole system, to the cycle of the five elements of metal, water, wood, fire and earth.

You will discover your sign in the Chinese zodiac, learn about the importance of symbolism in the practice of feng shui, and receive advice on the practical steps that you can take to prepare yourself and your home for implementing feng shui techniques.

Once you understand the concepts, you can apply them to any of the formulas, from the simplest Pa Kua method to the more advanced Flying Star formula, so it is well worth spending time familiarizing yourself with this section before you move on.

It is not difficult – it is simply a matter of appreciating that these concepts are the tools you need to help you make exciting and positive changes to your living space and that, as with every practical project, using the right tools makes all the difference to the result.

THE CONCEPT OF CHI

When you walk into anyone's home, you can usually sense if it is a happy or a sad home. What you are sensing is an invisible energy that flows through the environment, through buildings, and through the human body. The Chinese call this energy 'chi' – actually, the dragon's cosmic breath – and understanding the concept of chi is the essence of understanding feng shui.

Everyone has the ability to 'feel' this energy. Some have a more heightened awareness than others, but everyone has the potential to sense the quality of energy around them. Similarly, everyone generates energy, which may feel 'positive' or 'negative'. Homes with a strong, invigorating energy usually belong to strong, successful people. On the other hand, homes that exude a defeated or tired energy usually belong to rather more exhausted people. Homes can be friendly and warm, or cold, angry and hostile. There are kind homes and aggressive homes, lucky homes and unlucky homes. The more intense the energy, the easier it is to become aware of it.

Sometimes the energy of spaces is stronger than the combined energy of its residents, and other times the personality of the home owner dominates. But almost always the home (or office) will mirror and reflect the attitudes, directions, moods and well-being of its residents. It is only by tuning into energy that we can improve it. Develop awareness of the energy of your home, as this will help you to improve its feng shui by leaps and bounds.

It is very important to replenish the chi constantly and keep it moving (see pages 14–15). The energy of the home must never be allowed to stagnate. Energy is described as being either 'yang' or 'yin'. The concept of yang and yin is encapsulated in the symbol illustrated here – yang is the white part of the symbol and yin is the black part, but each part has a 'seed' of the other colour, signifying that everything has the potential to transform to its opposite. There is a constant exchange of chi between the two. Thus day changes to night, summer changes to winter, good changes to bad, and heaven changes to earth – and vice versa.

Yang is considered to be the masculine force in the Universe and is associated with

RIGHT This is the yin yang symbol, which in Chinese is known as the 'tai chi'. Think of individual rooms as small tai chi and your whole house as the big tai chi.

12

LEFT There is good yin/yang balance in this room and this ensures the 'tai chi' of the room is harmonious. The balance is evident in the use of colours and the placement of the furniture. In addition, the sofa provides good support.

south, summer, day, heat, sunshine, and with positive and powerful qualities. On the other hand, yin is considered to be the feminine force and is associated with north, winter, night, cold, wet, and with negative and passive qualities. In the Chinese agricultural almanac, heaven is at the height of summer and is very yang, while earth is in the middle of winter and is very yin.

Yang energy is what is needed to bring good fortune to a home. However, Chinese Taoist masters stress that yin and yang must be assessed according to their strength. Yang energy is either young yang or old yang. Yang energy that is 'old', or exhausted, tends to dissipate and transform into yin unless given a new lease of life. For homes to enjoy robust good fortune, the yang energy within should be young yang – fresh, strong and vital.

Chi must be kept moving all the time. When chi is quiet, it simply stagnates and attracts what is known as 'yin spirit formation' – a situation of chi energy that is interpreted by feng shui masters as being too still, quiet and dull, and hence with little power to attract good fortune. For good fortune of the material kind to be created there must be an abundant supply of yang energy. Yang chi is constantly moving, never coming to a standstill; only then can there be the vitality that contributes to continuous good fortune.

THE FLOW OF CHI

RIGHT The flow of chi determines its quality in the home. As much as possible let the chi meander rather than flow in a straight line, and always look at the room usage on both sides of each separating wall.

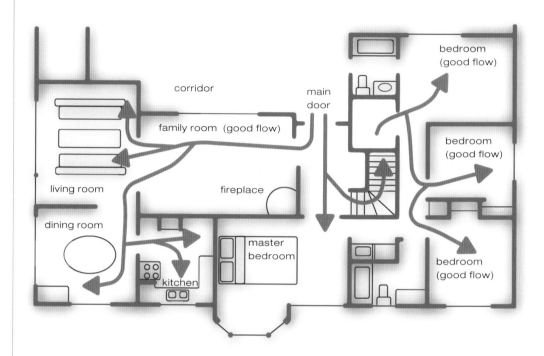

The speed and direction of the flow of chi is also significant. In the home it is really important to plan the layout of rooms and the placement of doors in such a way that the chi meanders through the house. If the chi is allowed to flow in a straight line, it gathers speed and takes on killing energy that harms the residents.

A meandering flow can be achieved by using plants, low furniture and room dividers such as sideboards and screens to slow down the chi. Because of this, feng shui is sometimes known as the art of placement. In the layout plan illustrated above, the flow of chi needs some feng shui improvement.

The chi flows straight from the door into the master bedroom. Residents in the room will suffer from straight energy, which is fierce and hostile. The best remedy is to hang paintings on the wall of the corridor.

Also note that the master bedroom shares a wall with the kitchen. This is not a desirable arrangement since fire chi from the kitchen can disturb sleep. In this case, however, the oven is placed on the opposite wall so the fire chi does not disturb the sleeping resident too badly.

The family room fireplace is located against the wall, which is also shared with the master bedroom. Again, this is not advisable, as fire chi so close to the bedroom causes yang disturbances, which could prevent residents sleeping well.

To keep the chi moving freely, it is always a good idea to move furniture – sofas, beds and small sideboards – in order to get at the dirt that accumulates beneath. This slight movement of furniture is very good feng shui medicine for the house. In addition to cleaning the spaces of the home, it moves the chi.

TIPS FOR CREATING A GOOD FLOW OF CHI

■ Open doors and windows daily, early in the morning, to suck in fresh air and winds from outside (you need to open at least two doors or windows to create the flow of chi).

■ Clean under the carpets regularly, since this moves the chi.

■ Move large cupboards to get at the dirt that accumulates behind.

■ Give the undersides of beds a good vacuuming to clear the space you sleep on.

■ At least once a year undertake 'spring cleaning'.

■ Have a programme of repainting the home once every two or three years.

■ Have a programme to revitalize the home through minor renovations.

■ Occasionally change the furniture of the home, or create a new arrangement of the furniture to give it a new lease of life.

CREATING FRESH NEW ENERGY

The revitalizing of interior space results in a very magical change of energy. Negative energy of any kind can be overcome by the practice of actively bringing in young, fresh new energy that has greater vitality, replenishes the home and keeps the chi inside robust and growing.

You can do this any time you wish – I usually choose the two weeks just before the lunar new year. In addition to cleaning the house throughout, you can include cleansing rituals, using bells, singing bowls and incense (see pages 146–47). These rituals generate positive shifts of the intangible forces that will enhance the energy of your home. They can also be used to help remove negative chi that may have come in to your house from neighbours or previous residents or through death or illness.

There are few things that bring faster results than using one's feng shui

knowledge to revitalize the home. It is helpful to look on feng shui enhancement as an ongoing process. Every time you make changes, you must be conscious that you are refreshing the energy by moving the chi.

You will find that houses always feel good after a well-planned feng shui renovation. It causes a rush of new chi into the home, which has the most revitalizing yang effect. The chi never gets a chance to stagnate. The energy of the home is therefore vital and alive and never becomes lethargic.

BELOW Use a seven-metal Tibetan singing bowl to create fresh new energy in the home. These singing bowls have the power to absorb and transform negative chi.

CREATING AN ENERGY FIELD

One of the most powerful protections for one's living space is the creation of a defensive field of guardian chi. This is done by developing the capability of focused mental imaging. Everyone has this ability, which involves concentration to create powerful visualizations in the mind. The images you build mentally have a mysterious power and this can be channelled towards creating a force field of energy that protects the home.

This force field works in different ways. It can prevent hostile chi from penetrating the natural aura of the home; it can stop people who have hidden bad intentions toward the residents from even entering the home; and it can act as a kind of invisible barrier against wandering spirits that coexist with us in a different realm. How powerful the force field that you build will be depends on the strength of the concentration you use to create it.

Generally, the more attuned you are to the energy of your home, the closer you will be to its spirit and therefore the more empowered your force field will be. Empowerment of this kind can never be used to harm people, and it works best when motivation is pure. For instance, the mental visualizations of parents who are motivated to protect their children carry great strength. This is because the energy behind the mental image is unconditional love, the spirit of which has great power. Those of you familiar with creative visualization or who have done some meditation will find it easy to create the force field.

It helps to have a picture in your mind of your home, over which you see the cocoon of blue light. Think of the light as a protective halo. If you live in an apartment, imagine the light encasing the whole building so that everyone within enjoys its benefits.

When you do this meditation regularly, your home will enjoy the harmony of being one with the cosmos. This is because you are channelling vital energy from the Universe into your home, making it vibrant and filled with strong yin/yang chi.

Visualization exercise

1 Stand in the centre of the room. Raise both arms high in front of you with palms open, facing outward. Take a deep 'in' breath as you raise your arms, and then gently let the palms of your hands lower a few inches. Breathe out. Do this three times to awaken the chi. Visualize receiving energy in the form of golden light from the Universe.

2 Hold your hands, palms open and facing the sky as if to receive this energy from the Universe. Feel the chi by tuning into the palms of your hands. Stay like this for a few minutes. When you feel a tingling sensation on your palms, slowly turn them to face each other. Keep your hands above your head.

3 Slowly lower your hands and imagine holding a transparent sphere of protective blueish light between the palms of your hands – hold this sphere of bright intense energy. Next move your palms very slowly away from each other and imagine the sphere of light getting larger and larger.

4 Now visualize the sphere of light energy getting brighter and bigger until it becomes bigger than you, bigger than the room, bigger than your house, your apartment … soon it surrounds the whole house or the whole apartment building with its protective light. Nothing negative can penetrate the force field created by this sphere of light.

Focus strongly on this protective aura around your home. Be convinced of its power. Now gently close your eyes and visualize the blue light completely cocooning your house, apartment or simply your room. Think, 'This is the energy field of my space/home/room. Nothing harmful can penetrate this energy field.'

THE EIGHT ASPIRATIONS

This is the easiest of feng shui methods. It combines the use of symbolism with the Pa Kua directions and the attributes of each room to activate the luck of eight aspirations. These aspirations relate to career growth, attainment of wealth, enjoying good health and family life, achieving recognition and fame, enjoying good children, attracting good marriage and romance luck, having good education luck and enjoying the patronage of powerful and influential people.

Feng shui is based on the premise that there are eight different kinds of 'luck' to which people aspire. Each of these aspirations is associated with a direction on the compass, and by enhancing the feng shui in that sector of the home, good fortune associated with the kind of luck you are activating will manifest – sometimes in ways you least expect!

One of the most potent systems for activating energy in homes is the Pa Kua method (see page 43–55). The Pa Kua is an eight-sided object, empowered by its trigrams. These three-lined symbols (made up of broken and unbroken lines, or a mixture of both, depending on their meaning in Chinese) are placed on each of its sides in two different arrangements, generally referred to as the Early Heaven and the Later Heaven arrangements. Feng shui is the skill of deciphering the meanings of these arrangements of the trigrams in different situations.

The eight aspirations of the Pa Kua method make use of the Later Heaven arrangement of the trigrams around the tai chi symbol. The trigrams arranged on each side of the Pa Kua assign elements and other associations to each of the eight sides. The placement of the trigrams around the Pa Kua indicate the sectors in a home suitable for each family member.

When any corner is cleverly and properly activated it causes the manifestation of the luck of that corner. This method of feng shui is easy but can be as powerful as the more complex formulas.

THE EIGHT ASPIRATIONS AND THEIR ASSOCIATED DIRECTIONS	
Career	north
Education	northeast
Health	east
Wealth	southeast
Fame	south
Romance	southwest
Children	west
Mentors	northwest

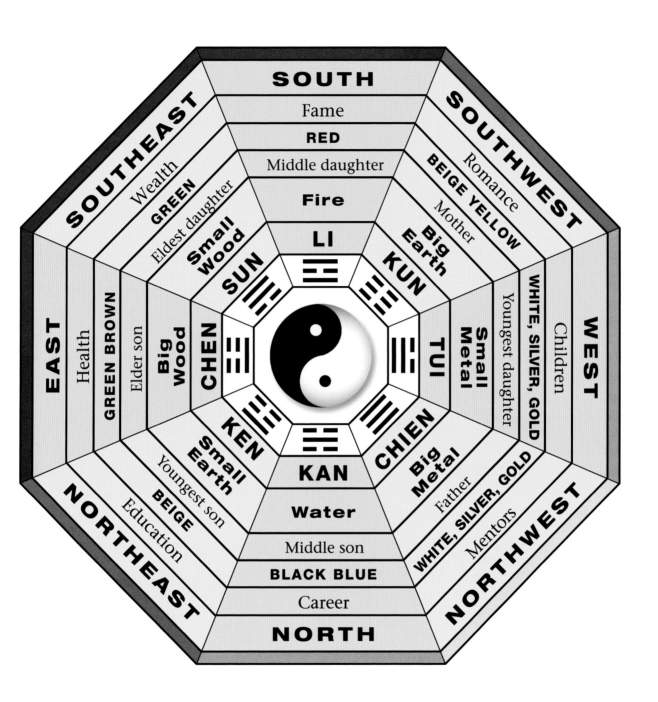

ABOVE This illustration shows a Pa Kua. Each compass direction on it is associated with an element such as fire, a family member and a colour. It also shows which objects or features, such as plants or ponds, can be used to activate the luck of each direction. It is one of the simplest forms of feng shui.

THE FIVE-ELEMENT THEORY

A core concept in feng shui practice is the theory of the five elements. If you thoroughly understand this concept (also known as wu xing in Chinese), you will become adept in feng shui and also gain a firm grounding in the fundamental philosophy of Chinese thought. Many things Chinese are based on wu xing, from fortune-telling to medical cures, healthy living, chi kung exercises and fighting martial arts.

BELOW The element of fire is excellent for activating the luck of recognition when placed in the south corner of the home. It is best represented as a bright light, a lamp or lanterns.

The five-elements theory is the foundation of all these esoteric skills. In feng shui, knowledge of the five elements theory and its three cycles – productive, exhausting and destructive – offers invaluable insights into the cures, remedies and energizers recommended by feng shui masters. It is thus an extremely good idea to commit the three cycles of the five elements to memory.

To use the theory of the five elements in feng shui, you will need to understand the relationships of each of the elements – fire, wood, water, metal and earth – to each other. There are three relationships and

THE FIVE ELEMENTS AND THEIR ASSOCIATIONS					
	WOOD	**WATER**	**FIRE**	**METAL**	**EARTH**
SEASON	spring	winter	summer	autumn	between
DIRECTION	east/southeast	north	south	west/northwest	southwest/northeast
COLOUR	green	black	red	white	ochre
SHAPE	rectangle	wavy	triangle	circle	square
ENERGY	outwards	descending	upwards	inwards	sideways
NUMBERS	3, 4	1	9	6, 7	2, 5, 8

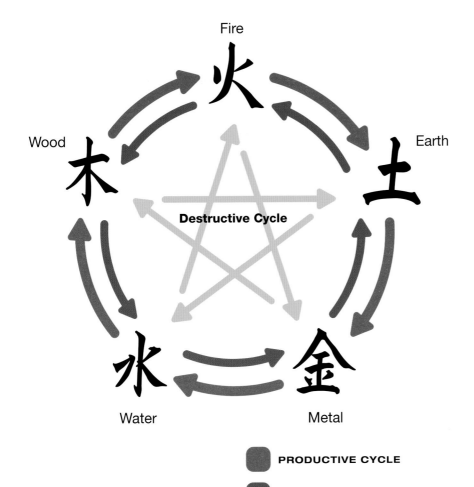

Fire

火

Wood

木

Earth

土

Destructive Cycle

Water

水

Metal

金

■ **PRODUCTIVE CYCLE**

■ **EXHAUSTING CYCLE**

■ **DESTRUCTIVE CYCLE**

LEFT This diagram shows the three cycles of the five elements in their relationships to each other. For example, in the destructive cycle we can see that metal destroys wood and wood destroys earth but in the productive cycle wood produces fire and water produces wood and so on.

these give rise to the three cycles. These are illustrated in the diagram.

■ To energize or enhance corners of the Pa Kua, use the productive cycle of the five elements to strengthen.

■ To install remedies and cures for afflicted chi in the corners of the Pa Kua, use the exhausting cycle.

■ To completely overcome and control killing chi, use the destructive cycle.

The importance of the five-element theory in planning your life auspiciously becomes increasingly obvious as you go through this book. The key to using it is to know the element of each direction as shown on the illustration on page 19. This is the basis upon which all feng shui cures and remedies are devised. Try to ensure that the element of each corner does not get hurt, so for example, placing water in the south is water putting out the fire, but placing wood in the south will fan the fire. In the same way, a lamp placed in the earth corners enhances these sectors while plants will hurt them.

ELEMENT SYMBOLS

Each of the five elements can be
represented by features and symbols
that can add to the beauty and sense
of harmony of the home, as well as
enhancing and energizing the luck sectors.

Water features for water energy

The best enhancer for the north, and
to attract prosperity luck by activating
the east and southeast, is a water feature.
This need not be large or elaborate, nor be
stocked with expensive fish. In feng shui,
however, distinction is made between yin
water, which is quiet and still with neither
fish nor plants in it, and yang water which
is moving and filled with life chi. Thus,
yang water is usually oxygenated, has
fish, or has plants growing within.

  To activate for prosperity luck it is
important you use only yang water as
energizers. In recent years, water features
of every variety have been made available
as more and more people become aware
of the great benefits of feng shui.

Crystals for earth energy

The best way to enhance earth energy is
with crystals, which are truly 'of the earth'
and the most powerful manifestation of
earth energy. These are particularly
appropriate in the southwest, which is the
romance sector. Two lovely large pieces of
rose quartz – or two rose-quartz hearts – are
perfect here, especially as this is the crystal
associated with unconditional love and the
heart chakra. The northeast is also an earth
element sector, and here a clear quartz
crystal globe will attract scholarship luck
and greatly enhance your children's
academic achievements.

Plants for wood energy

An excellent way to represent the wood
element in the east and southeast, and to
activate the fire element in the south, is
with plants. Live young plants are symbolic
of growth upward and outward. It is very
important that the plants look lush and
healthy, so you need to make sure that you
keep them well-watered and fed – dead or

dying plants will not create auspicious chi. Young broad-leaved plants are ideal, and flowering plants will represent the blossoming of your projects.

Lights for fire energy

Lighting is one of the most powerful feng shui tools – few others can match its potency. In the corners of the room that benefit from fire energy (south, northeast and southwest) it is a good idea to keep the lights turned on all through the day and night.

■ Bright lights in the south bring fame and recognition.

■ Bright lights in the southwest bring love, romance and family joyous occasions.

LEFT AND OPPOSITE These are examples of objects that signify the elements. In feng shui you can be as creative as you wish in the use of elements, though remember never to overdo things. Too much fire burns you while too much water can drown you. Balance and harmony are vital when designing one's space.

■ Bright lights in the northeast bring the luck of scholarship.

■ Candles are also excellent for representing the fire element.

Wind chimes for metal energy

Coins are an excellent way to represent metal energy in the west and northwest and to energize the water element in the north. Three gold Chinese coins tied together with red string or ribbon to represent energizing fire energy are perfect. You can also use all-metal wind chimes, metal vases or bowls, or even place your metal stereo equipment in these sectors to activity the metal energy.

23

CHINESE ASTROLOGY

Chinese astrology uses a person's day, hour, month and year of birth to chart his or her destiny. The year is also used in feng shui. It determines the zodiac animal sign that assigns each person an element and a Kua number. These can then be used to work out individuals' good and bad luck locations.

The Chinese zodiac is divided into 12 time periods, but unlike the Western zodiac, which is divided into periods of approximately one month, each of the 12 animals in the Chinese zodiac reigns for a whole year, starting at the lunar new year in late January or early February. The zodiac animals are the Rat, the Ox, the Tiger, the Rabbit, the Dragon, the Snake, the Horse, the Goat, the Monkey, the Rooster, the Dog and the Pig. The table below shows you which animal is

Year of the Rat (Water)

1924, 1936, 1948, 1960, 1972, 1984, 1996, 2008

Year of the Ox (Earth)

1925, 1937, 1949, 1961, 1973, 1985, 1997, 2009

Year of the Tiger (Wood)

1926, 1938, 1950, 1962, 1974, 1986, 1998, 2010

Year of the Rabbit (Wood)

1927, 1939, 1951, 1963, 1975, 1987, 1999, 2011

Year of the Dragon (Earth)

1928, 1940, 1952, 1964, 1976, 1988, 2000, 2012

Year of the Snake (Fire)

1929, 1941, 1953, 1965, 1977, 1989, 2001, 2013

associated with your year of birth. If you were born before the lunar new year, you are associated with the animal from the previous year, so for example, if you were born on 2 January 1946 you come under the astrological sign of the Rooster. Each animal is also associated with one of the five elements, which is also shown on the table. When planning your feng shui, you can work with your zodiac sign and your personal element to help you get the best luck chi.

The zodiac also enables you to calculate Kua numbers (see pages 59–60) which will reveal your auspicious and inauspicious directions. It is the Kua number that enables you to use the element theories, the directions and the symbols to bring you into harmony with your environment and open up the world of personalized feng shui. The Kua number also reveals the directions that bring you the best kind of wealth, romance, personal development and health luck. It also reveals whether your home is in sync with your personal energy. In the same way the Kua number also tells you which directions will harm you, bring you bad luck or cause you to attract enemies or total loss.

Knowing how to use the compass directions is known as the practice of Eight Mansions feng shui (see pages 56–65). By simply practising Eight Mansions feng shui, you will see immediate positive changes come into your life.

Year of the Horse (Fire)

1930, 1942, 1954, 1966, 1978, 1990, 2002, 2014

Year of the Sheep (Earth)

1931, 1943, 1955, 1967, 1979, 1991, 2003, 2015

Year of the Monkey (Metal)

1932, 1944, 1956, 1968, 1980, 1992, 2004, 2016

Year of the Rooster (Metal)

1933, 1945, 1957, 1969, 1981, 1993, 2005, 2017

Year of the Dog (Earth)

1934, 1946, 1958, 1970, 1982, 1994, 2006, 2018

Year of the Pig (Water)

1935, 1947, 1959, 1971, 1983, 1995, 2007, 2019

FENG SHUI SYMBOLISM

The practice of feng shui is based on adopting a defensive strategy. This protects your home and office from being affected by 'killing chi', which creates bad feng shui and can negate all your efforts to activate and enhance your good feng shui.

Feng shui prescribes many methods of protection, ranging from the simple placement of guardian images to the more complex application of symbolic cures used in conjunction with formula feng shui. There are different types of killing chi, requiring different kinds of protection and cures. Bad chi can occur because of hostile structures or be caused by invisible, intangible forces. Bad feng shui can be caused by imbalances in the yin/yang chi of the space. Feng shui teaches you to recognize when it is necessary to implement remedies to dispel bad luck and overcome energy that causes misfortunes.

Symbolism plays a big role in feng shui practice and many symbols are used as remedies and solutions to a range of feng shui ills. The Chinese have a variety of symbols and deities, known as 'celestial guardians'.

■ **ZHONG KUEI** (or Chong Kuei) protects against bad spirit harm. He is usually depicted carrying a sword in his right hand and a flask of wine in his left.

RIGHT Kuan Kong, the Chinese God of War, is considered a powerful guardian of feng shui.

He has a fierce countenance and he loves to drink, but he is also alert and mindful to the quality of the energy around him. Merely having his image in your home or office is sufficient to chase away the 'devils' (people who harbour ill intentions toward you).

■ **KUAN KONG**, especially the five-dragons Kuan Kong, is a wrathful deity, valued because he is said to protect you both physically and spiritually. Kuan Kong also protects wealth.

■ **DRAGONS, TORTOISES, PHOENIXES AND TIGERS** feature prominently in the practice of feng shui. These creatures are the four celestial guardians of any yin or yang abode. In the outer environment they are said to represent the hills and mountains that surround a building. Inside the home, they are powerfully propitious symbols in their own right, apart from the white tiger, which is best kept at a safe distance. Of the four, the dragon is the most prominent and significant. Indeed, the dragon is one of the most auspicious symbols of all, and having his image in the home always attracts good yang energy. Tortoises are also very important, and as protector images they are believed by many to be even better. Place tortoises in the north and preferably in the back half of your house, but not in the kitchen. Dragon Tortoises are a powerful combination of the two creatures, creating the courage chi of the dragon and the protective chi of the tortoise.

■ Other protective images include a pair of Fu dogs, a pair of Chi Lin – a mythical creature, with the head of a dragon, body of a horse and scales of a fish – other fierce animals and the powerful Door Gods.

Place celestial guardians correctly

Symbols of protection must be placed in the correct locations. The key area is at or near the entrance door. This is the mouth of the home, where chi enters. You can place a Kuan Kong image in the hallway, just inside the door – with his fierce countenance facing the door and looking directly at all who enter, it is said that even the most hardened ghosts and robbers get scared off! A five-dragons Kuan Kong, made of metal and either standing or seated, is also a very powerful cure for many Flying Star afflictions (see pages 93–95). These afflictions are usually associated with the earth element, which can be controlled effectively with metal energy.

Near the main door is a great place to hang an image of Zhong Kuei or images of the Door Gods. It is also at the door that a pair of Fu dogs or Chi Lin are most effective in their role as protective guardians. Placed one on either side, these celestials create excellent protection against harmful people, being cheated and petty burglary. Fu dogs and Chi Lin can be placed on floor level or raised.

For apartments they should be placed just outside, on either side of the door into the apartment. If your entrance door faces the lift, this is crucial to protect you from the symbolic attacking chi that emerges from the lift shaft. For homes in grounds with gates, the Fu dogs should be placed high up on top of the gate, looking out. This also attracts good fortune.

Do not have too many protective symbols unless your space is very big. Always relate to the size of your space. Balance is vital.

LEFT The Dragon Tortoise sitting on a bed of coins signifies protection and prosperity. The little baby tortoise carried on its back symbolizes good feng shui for the next generation too.

BELOW Fu dogs are excellent when placed on either side of entrance doors. Place the female dog (with baby dog) on the right hand side facing outwards, and place the male dog (with the globe) on the left side facing outwards.

COMPASS FENG SHUI

Authentic Chinese feng shui always uses the compass. Advanced practitioners use the Lo Pan – the feng shui compass – which contains many of the powerful compass formulas. For the amateur practitioner, however, a Western compass is sufficient.

ABOVE It is essential to use a proper compass to take directions. Accuracy is vital in the practice of feng shui.

The Eight Mansions formula uses charts (see page 65) that show the luck distribution of a building and how the luck changes according to the facing direction of the main door. These charts are not to be confused with the charts used in the Trigram and Flying Star formulas. In the Flying Star formula you must determine the facing direction of the house itself and not just the direction of the door.

To determine the facing direction of your house, you must use a compass. It is useful to invest in a good compass – try to obtain a reliable and accurate one that has the degrees marked out clearly. Make sure to take accurate readings – in fact, for feng shui purposes it is a good idea to take at least three readings for accuracy.

In most cases the facing direction of the house is taken at the main door, standing inside and facing squarely outward. This is usually the direction where the main road is – the source of maximum yang energy.

However, sometimes the house may be facing one direction while the door faces another. Generally, you have to decide the facing direction by looking at it and selecting from several possible criteria. Thus the facing direction of the house can be:

■ The direction of the main road, if the main door is on the side of the house facing a garage or a wall.

■ The direction where there is a big window giving the most unencumbered view.

■ The direction facing lower ground, where there might be a patio looking out.

■ The direction facing the driveway into the house.

It is not usually a problem to work out the facing direction of a house or bungalow, but for apartment buildings, where there is more than one entrance, it can be tricky. Look for the direction that faces the road or the view and use this as the facing direction of the building or of your house. If in doubt, analyze a couple of charts to see which one best describes the present luck of your house.

Once you know the facing direction of your door and house, you can determine its sitting direction, which is the direct opposite of the facing direction. So, when the house faces north it is sitting south; when it faces east it is sitting west, and so on. You are now ready to use the formula charts of compass feng shui.

AUSPICIOUS DIRECTIONS IN EIGHT MANSIONS FENG SHUI

The Eight Mansions feng shui charts show how luck is distributed in the different areas of a building. This is part of the Kua formula of personalized good and bad directions of individuals. The facing and sitting directions are vitally important when you use the Kua formula for personalizing feng shui (see pages 59–61). Indeed, the best usage of the Eight Mansions Kua directions in the home is in the arrangement and placement of furniture so that each resident can tap into their own personal 'auspicious' directions. When we talk about 'auspicious' directions, we are referring to both your facing and your sitting directions. It is important to be very clear which direction you are tapping when you make any new arrangement to your sitting direction and location.

Sometimes, both your sitting and facing directions are good for you. For instance, if you sit south you are facing north, so both directions are good for you if you are an east group person. (The concept of east and west groups is explained on page 61.) Likewise, if you sit northeast and are facing southwest, then, for a west group person, both the sitting and facing directions are good for you.

Sometimes, however, only one of the sitting/facing directions will be good for you; for example when you face west you will be sitting east and when you face northwest you will be sitting southeast. These sitting/facing directions are in conflict, since they belong to different groups of directions. In such situations, the facing direction carries more weight, so when faced with a dilemma, go with the facing direction.

LEFT Sit facing your best direction to help attract a good future.

UNDERSTANDING THE LO SHU SQUARE

The Lo Shu square is one of the most powerful of the feng shui symbols to have been revealed to the West in recent years. It is this square – a three by three grid of numbers – that enables a feng shui practitioner to unlock the secrets of the Pa Kua and the Lo Pan compass formulas.

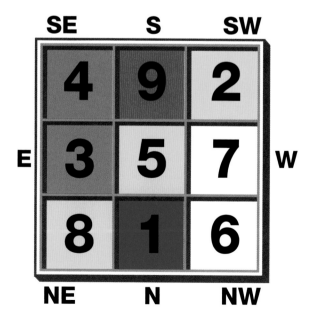

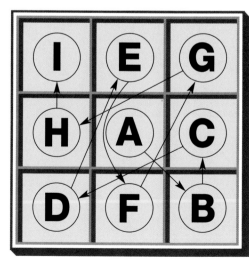

BELOW This is the Lo Shu square of nine numbers arranged with number 5 in the centre. The square unlocks many of the advanced formulas of feng shui. Compass directions and colours associated with each number are also shown. Beside it is a diagram illustrating the 'flight of numbers', described on page 31.

To understand the Lo Shu square look at the illustration below. Study the placement of the numbers in each of the nine sections and note the following: the central number is 5 and is an earth number that separates the lower and higher numbers; any three numbers in horizontal, vertical or diagonal lines add up to 15.

Lo Shu numbers and directions

The Lo Shu square is what gives a number to each of the eight directions of the Pa Kua. Thus the number 9 is designated as

the number of the south direction, and the number 1 is designated as the number of the north direction. Here are the numbers of all eight of the compass directions: 9 is south, 1 is north, 3 is east, 7 is west, 2 is southwest, 8 is northeast, 4 is southeast and 6 is northwest (see illustration below left). Note that since 5 is the centre number it does not have a corresponding compass direction.

The number that corresponds to each of the directions is derived by superimposing the Lo Shu square and its numbers onto the

Pa Kua. These numbers indicate the numerical energy of sectors. When combined with the five elements, you can see that:

■ You place one water feature in the north because the number here is one and water is the element of the north.

■ You place six rod wind chimes in the northwest because 6 is the number here and its element is metal.

■ You place a pair of crystal ducks in the southwest because the number here is 2 and its element is earth (thus crystals).

■ You place eight crystals in the northeast because 8 is the number here and the element is also earth.

■ You place seven coins in the west because the number here is 7 and metal is its element.

■ You place nine lanterns in the south because the element here is fire and the number here is 9.

■ You place four plants in the southeast because here the number is 4 and the element is wood.

■ You place three plants in the east because the number 3 and the element is wood.

Lo Shu numbers and colours

In the same way that there is a correlation between numbers and compass directions and elements there is also a relationship between numbers and colours. Thus 1 is shown in blue; 9 is shown in red; the numbers 3 and 4 are shown in green; the

numbers 6 and 7 in white, and the numbers 2 and 8 in yellow.

The Lo Shu numbers and symbolism

In addition to the symbolism of numbers and their relationship with the directions, elements and colours, it is also significant to see how, by following the movement of the numbers from the centre into each of the squares using the ascending numbers as a guide, you can see a symbol forming (see illustration above). Look at the 5 in the centre becoming 6 in the northwest; then 7 in the west, then jumping across to the northeast as 8, and jumping again to the south as 9, to the north as 1, then to the southwest as 2, and then to the east as 3 and to the southeast as 4. In the second illustration on page 30 this is shown as the movement from A to B to C and so forth.

This movement of the numbers is also known as the 'flight of the numbers'. This is the way that the numbers fly from square to square and that enables you to create a map of luck for any building during any period of time as long as the centre Lo Shu number for any year, month or day is known.

USING THE POWERFUL FORMULAS

Once you have familiarized yourself with the basic Pa Kua method of feng shui on pages 42–55, you can move on to the more powerful methods, and use them to help you gain control of your life by working with your personal directions and elements. Here is a brief introduction to the three formulas, which are explained in detail later in the book.

The three most powerful formulas are:

1. The Eight Mansions formula (see pages 56–65)

This is a personalized formula, which divides everyone into either east or west group people. East and west group people have auspicious and inauspicious directions, numbers, trigrams and houses. Thus there are west group numbers and directions just as there are east group numbers and directions. The formula states that, based on your lunar year of birth and your gender, it is possible to calculate your

Kua number. Based on the Kua number, it is then possible to know the following:

■ whether you are an east or west group person

■ which are your auspicious and inauspicious directions

■ which is your personal lucky trigram

■ which is your personal lucky number

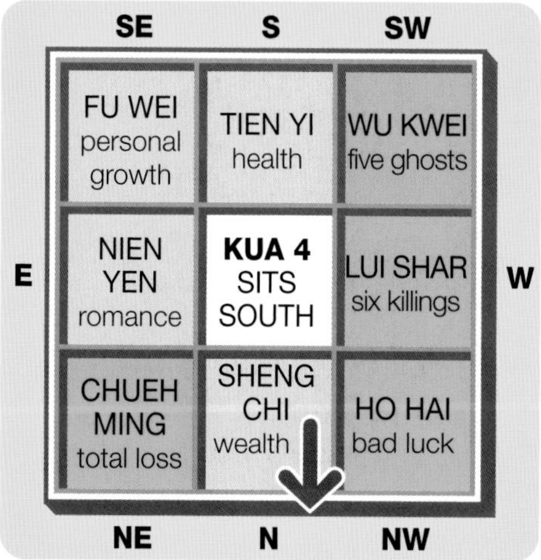

Knowing Eight Mansions enables you to practise very potent personalized feng shui. Armed with only a compass and the above information, you can select houses, rooms, directions and corners that bring maximum luck. Moreover, you can take steps to ensure that you are protected from inadvertently living in unsuitable houses, staying in inauspicious rooms and facing unlucky directions.

2. The House Trigram formula (see pages 66–81)

Under the House Trigram formula, houses are categorized as one of eight types, with

RIGHT Shown here is an example of an Eight Mansions chart. The black arrow shows the direction the house faces. The blue coloured squares show the four good directions and the red squares show the four unlucky directions.

SE	S	SW
FU WEI personal growth	TIEN YI health	WU KWEI five ghosts
NIEN YEN romance	KUA 4 SITS SOUTH	LUI SHAR six killings
CHUEH MING total loss	SHENG CHI wealth	HO HAI bad luck

E / W, NE / N / NW

The little numbers on the top left hand corner are mountain stars. These reveal the relationship luck of each of the corners.

The little numbers on the top right hand corner are water stars. These reveal the wealth luck of each of the corners.

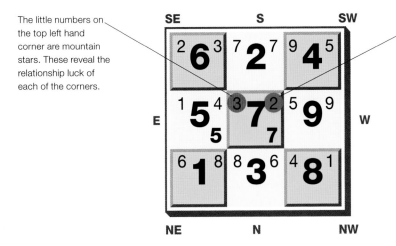

each type being named after one of the eight trigrams. This method is based on the sitting direction of a house (see page 28). The trigram of the house determines the chart of the house. This chart is then used in combination with the Flying Star annual and monthly charts to alert house residents of bad combinations of stars that bring illness, sickness and loss. This method of feng shui is excellent for keeping up to date on killing chi energy, which is created by the sheer passage of time. The House Trigram formula is used in conjunction with the Eight Mansions formula to determine the compatibility of houses with their residents, based on their personal Kua numbers.

3. The Flying Star formula (see pages 82–109)

This is the powerful formula that reveals the transformation of luck in any living space from period to period and enables you to plan your life accordingly. This formula identifies various types of good and bad luck in the Nine Palaces of any home, including identifying illness and loss

stars. The Nine Palaces are the rooms in the home demarcated according to compass directions.

The formula is based on the numbers of the Lo Shu square and it involves numerology in feng shui – knowing what the numbers 1 to 9 mean and what number combinations indicate. When you read a Flying Star natal chart you will discover how effective feng shui can be, and when you design your space according to the information given in these charts, at the very least you will definitely be protected from bad feng shui. The Flying Star formula is especially powerful when used in conjunction with the Eight Mansions Kua formula and symbolic (Taoist) feng shui.

USE YOUR OWN JUDGEMENT

There will be many instances when the different formulas seem to offer different advice. This is where you will need to use your own judgement. Where it is not possible to meet all criteria select the advice that is more easy to implement.

TIME INFLUENCES ON FENG SHUI

In the past, the powerful practice of Flying Star feng shui was not widely known. This was mainly because it was kept secret by the masters and also required the thousand-year calendar and the formula to create the charts. Today Flying Star has become increasingly available.

In recent years a great deal of feng shui knowledge has been revealed, including information about the annual and monthly charts that can be drawn up to investigate the luck of different houses.

On pages 36–37 you will see how I have simplified the thousand-year calendar (also known as the HSIA calendar) into two tables that enable anyone with a brief knowledge of Flying Star charts to look up the Lo Shu numbers relevant for each year and each month, and from there work out the charts. This is truly a breakthrough!

The annual and monthly charts are always presented in the same format as the Lo Shu grid. An annual chart simply shows which of the nine numbers rules each of the eight direction sectors in any given year or any given month. By looking at the numbers and knowing their meanings, we will know whether they bring good or bad luck to the sector. This in effect offers us an early-warning system of potential bad luck coming in the form of illness, burglaries or accidents, and enables us to put remedies in place and also take extra care.

This is the most exciting part of time-dimension feng shui and is what makes it such a valuable living skill. Simply by generating the charts for any month or year, we are able to tell whether the bedroom or the office, for example, will have good chi energy or illness chi energy. The accompanying tables of meanings on pages 72–80 can be referred to for analysis.

It is exactly the same process for the daily or even hourly charts. By referring to the relevant Lo Shu numbers for each hour or day, we can generate more numbers to explain the luck of that hour. Obviously, it would be a most tedious process working out the analysis of every hour, but this will give you an idea of how the ancient court astrologers used to work, safeguarding the Emperor, the son of heaven.

The way the annual and monthly charts are created is based on the ruling Lo Shu number of the year or the month. Ruling Lo Shu numbers for the year, month, day and hour are part of the Chinese Almanac. From this number, charts are created simply by placing the ruling number in the centre of the square and from there, using the flight pattern of the original Lo Shu square (see page 30), we can fill in all the numbers of the other sectors. So the key is to obtain the centre number of the year or month.

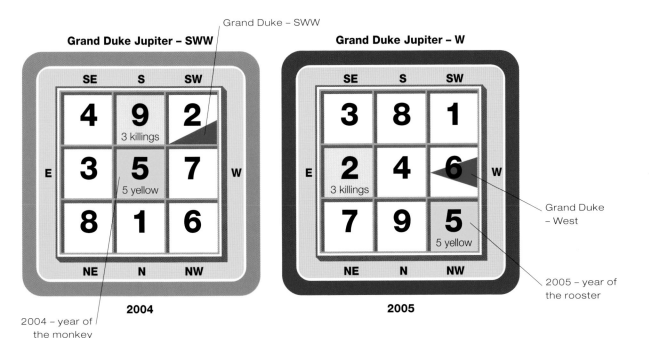

Grand Duke – SWW

Grand Duke Jupiter – SWW

SE	S	SW
4	9	2
	3 killings	
3	5	7
E	5 yellow	W
8	1	6
NE	N	NW

2004

2004 – year of the monkey

Grand Duke Jupiter – W

SE	S	SW
3	8	1
2	4	6
3 killings		W
7	9	5
		5 yellow
NE	N	NW

2005

Grand Duke – West

2005 – year of the rooster

To give you an idea of how the luck of various rooms changes over time, I have shown the annual Lo Shu charts for 2004 and 2005, with the afflicted locations indicated (above). The number 5 is the ruling number for 2004, so 5 has been placed in the centre of the chart. The 2004 chart reveals that in this year the auspicious sector of the house would be the northeast which favours scholars.

If your front door or your bedroom is placed in the northeast then you will enjoy good fortune during the year. Unfortunately the number 5, which is known as the deadly five yellow (see page 102), has flown into the centre grid and this brings a year of some misfortune to those whose luck cycle is at a low ebb. It is vital to place metal energy (metal wind chimes, for instance) in the centre of the home. In 2004 since the illness star 2 has flown into the southwest it is beneficial to place metal windchimes here all

through the year. In the year 2004 it is also not advisable to sit facing the southwest direction as the Grand Duke Jupiter resides here (see page 101). It is also not advisable to undertake or start renovations in the Southwest.

However, in 2005 the illness star has flown to the east which is also the location of the three killings (see page 103). In 2005 the east direction is afflicted and if your main door or bedroom is located here, it does spell some misfortune. The use of metal energy (but not wind chimes – this would activate the three killings) would be beneficial. The deadly five yellow flies to the northwest bringing bad luck here, and also to the patriarch of the family.

In 2005 the best luck sector would be the south. So if your bedroom or main door is in the south you would have a very good year indeed. This is because the number 8 is a very lucky number from 2004 to 2024.

ABOVE You can see from the annual charts that the sector with the best luck is northeast in 2004 and south in 2005. This is because these are occupied by the most auspicious of the numbers – number 8.

THE LO SHU NUMBERS FOR THE YEARS 2001 TO 2023	
YEAR	**REIGNING NUMBER**
2001	8
2002	7
2003	6
2004	5
2005	4
2006	3
2007	2
2008	1
2009	9
2010	8
2011	7
2012	6
2013	5
2014	4
2015	3
2016	2
2017	1
2018	9
2019	8
2020	7
2021	6
2022	5
2023	4

THE FENG SHUI HOROSCOPE

You can use the table on the left here to find out the ruling Lo Shu number of any given year and from there cast an annual Lo Shu chart for the year. This gives you the luck map for any building or house for that year.

Until very recently few people were aware of how easy it is to create the annual Lo Shu chart. The equivalent Lo Shu number for each year is always given in the Chinese Almanac, from where the table shown on the left was extracted. This table enables you to cast your own feng shui horoscope charts for each year based on the annual number, which is also known as the 'reigning' number.

You can combine the annual number with the Trigram charts on page 70 to see how the annual numbers (known as flying stars) affect each of the rooms in your house. You can then use the tables of meanings on pages 72–80 to analyze the effects of these numbers. You can also use the mountain and water flying stars (see pages 82–109), to give you even more information about the good and bad luck areas of your home. These combinations also apply to monthly chart numbers of each of the sectors. This way you will know the luck of your own home/shop/office in any month. Try it out – you will be surprised at how accurate it is. For instance, when the monthly and annual 8 converges in the sector where you have the front door of your shop, you will find sales shooting up. When the 5 converges, on the other hand, sales are sure to take a drop – unless you put remedies into place! Here lies the great benefit of knowing time-dimension feng shui.

In the example illustrated below left, in the year 2005 the reigning number is 4, so the Lo Shu square created for that year is based on 4 being the central number. Try to work out how the 2005 chart is made. See how the next number, 5, is placed in the northwest and then the next number 6 is in the west and so on. This placing of the numbers follows the sequence of directions exactly the same way as the original Lo Shu square on page 30, which has 5 in its centre.

This is known as the 'flight of the numbers' in the Lo Shu square. The flight pattern is really very simple, and when you understand it you will have learnt the basis of Flying Star charts and will be set to use one of the more complex compass formulas.

RIGHT This chart is the Lo Shu chart for 2005, with number 4 in the centre. Every year the numbers move around the square in the pattern known as the flight of numbers.

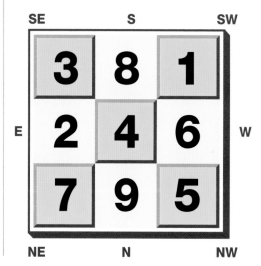

	SE	S	SW
	3	8	1
E	2	4	6	W
	7	9	5
	NE	N	NW

MONTHLY FENG SHUI HOROSCOPE

Once you have mastered the annual star numbers and learnt how to draw up the charts for each year, you are ready to move on to the monthly charts. Again, here you use the reigning Lo Shu numbers. These will be the reigning numbers for the different months. The calendar used is the HSIA calendar, which is different from the lunar calendar, so that each year the first month starts on 4 February, which is described as the Lap Chun – the first day of spring. Sometimes it starts on 5 February, but the dates indicating the start of each of the HSIA calendar months are fairly accurate. The precious table below enables anyone to create the chart for any month at all for the next thousand years!

Once you know the monthly numbers of each sector of the grid chart that represents your home, you will be able to do advanced feng shui work on your interiors. If you find it hard to understand all this at first, please do persevere. It is not difficult, but you do need to concentrate. This is part of the theory of feng shui science using the compass and the Lo Pan. It is a very powerful formula for fine-tuning the feng shui of your home, your office or your shop, and you can use it to find out why you had such good luck in some months and why in other months so many things seemed to go wrong. The vital thing is to apply remedies to overcome the bad numbers when they fly into each of the sectors.

LO SHU NUMBERS FOR DIFFERENT MONTHS IN DIFFERENT YEARS

MONTH	START OF MONTH	Lo shu number in YEAR of RAT, RABBIT, HORSE & ROOSTER	Lo shu number in YEAR of DOG, SHEEP, DRAGON & OX	Lo shu number in YEAR of TIGER, SNAKE, PIG & MONKEY
1	4 February	8	5	2
2	6 March	7	4	1
3	5 April	6	3	9
4	6 May	5	2	8
5	6 June	4	1	7
6	7 July	3	9	6
7	8 August	2	8	5
8	8 September	1	7	4
9	8 October	9	6	3
10	7 November	8	5	2
11	7 December	7	4	1
12	6 January	6	3	9

Note: The dates may have a variation of plus or minus one day. The above is the summary of the thousand-year calendar, which should be consulted for more accurate analysis of the luck according to months and years.

BEFORE YOU START

The best way to practise feng shui is to start by seeing 'the big picture'. Look at the overall impression and examine the external surroundings of your home before going into the details. Take photographs that show you the home from all angles.

You will be surprised at what the camera captures that your naked eye had missed. For instance, if you stand at your main door and photograph the view directly facing you, you will be able to identify obstacles and physical afflictions immediately. The best view to have is of a flat field or open ground of some kind. When you detect harmful, hostile objects outside, always create protection for your door by blocking the view or reflecting it away.

Tuning in to the pattern and flow of chi inside any living space requires nothing more than focusing one's concentration. As you stand at the main door facing out, try to get a feel for whether the energy coming at you is benevolent or agitated. In feng shui terminology, benevolent chi is generally referred to as sheng chi – the dragon's cosmic breath. Harmful or killing chi is referred to as shar chi. Good chi can also be wang chi, which is ripening chi, and bad chi can also be negative or dead chi. Developing awareness will enable you to design different kinds of good energy for the interiors of your home.

Draw a plan

Always refer to a floor plan when you are doing the feng shui of any home, to enable you to see where each room is

RIGHT This is a modern clutter-free kitchen which has a wonderful flow of chi. When your kitchen has good feng shui, the health of the family is robust and strong.

placed in relation to the others. You also need a good floor plan to show you how energy flows within the house. When you survey the inside of the home, develop awareness of shapes, colours, lines, dimensions and the placement of objects and furniture. Note if rooms are welcoming or whether the energy is putting you off. You will be surprised at how many things you used to not notice.

Clear clutter

Almost all feng shui practitioners agree that clutter in the home does not attract good feng shui – in fact, clutter causes luck to become severely blocked, so that success luck will be hard to come by. So before you start learning about the different feng shui formulas and how to implement them, clear the clutter from your home.

Homes do not need to be as clinical as a hospital, but when living rooms and bedrooms are allowed to pile up high with old newspapers and magazines, dirty clothes and so forth, the flow of energy is certain to be blocked. Just as the flow of chi in the human body must not get blocked, as it will cause illness, so also the chi in the home should flow smoothly, unimpeded. When the energy of the home gets sick, it affects the residents' luck as well.

Clearing clutter can actually be very therapeutic. Try it some time when you are feeling lethargic. Clear your desk, file all your letters and notes and throw away all the junk that accumulates over time, and as you do so feel your energy getting lighter and brighter. In the bedroom, where clothes tend to choke up wardrobe space and stuff swept under the bed can cause all sorts of bad feng shui to manifest for the sleeping couple, spend time

clearing the clutter. Throw out old and out-of-date clothes. Unless you make room for new clothes, your energy will remain static.

Taoist feng shui masters always advocate making space for new things to come into one's life. This is why they never like rice urns to be full to the brim – there should always be some room for new opportunities and new goodies to enter one's life. Clearing clutter implies making way for new energy to flow through.

In the kitchen, space must really be kept absolutely clean and clear of clutter. Never leave food lying on table tops and keep rubbish bins closed to avoid unpleasant smells. Do not attract creepy crawlies as this brings negative energy into the kitchen. Nothing hurts feng shui like stale food and dirty, unwashed plates and dishes. The kitchen illustrated on the left is not only uncluttered, it is also clean and happy-looking. The food is cooked within a clean and auspicious environment. Try to achieve an uncluttered and happy atmosphere in every room in your home.

ABOVE Shown here is a rather cluttered kitchen. In such a situation, chi energy is confused. As well as clearing clutter, it would also help to remove the plates lining the walls near the ceiling.

CLEARING BASIC CONFUSIONS

The prevalence of different systems of feng shui has led to some confusion in the minds of practitioners, especially in recent years when interest in feng shui has led to a veritable explosion of books on the subject.

Confusion generally revolves around which feng shui method of investigation to use, as well as issues such as how directions are taken under different systems, what symbols are used and how they are to be placed, and what advice to follow when confronted with contradictory recommendations. When sifting through all the basic issues of contention that cause confusion, it is important to remember that feng shui is both a science and an art – sometimes requiring technical investigations and complex calculations and at other times requiring an almost instinctive selection of options. Feng shui is mostly a diagnostic practice requiring judgement, experience and a good dose of common sense.

Using feng shui today means adapting classical and traditional practice to a modern environment. Theory alone is not good enough – theory alone is an impractical approach. Unless feng shui theory is interpreted with an eye to the urban landscapes of modern city living, the practice of feng shui cannot bring meaningful results. So there is a need to interpret and adapt feng shui guidelines to suit modern-day living and work spaces.

Some common issues causing confusion that need to be clarified include the following:

1. Taking directions

When practising formula feng shui, a proper compass should be used. Note that directions referred to in feng shui texts always mean directions as taken with a compass, not from the front door, not from where the sun sets or rises, and not from whether you live in the northern or southern hemisphere. Directions are always taken with a compass. Yang dwellings, such as houses and offices (a description of the yang symbol associations and qualities is

found on pages 12–13), can be taken with any good Western-style compass. Please note that feng shui charts are always shown with south at the top.

2. Which direction to take
To practise Eight Mansions feng shui, the direction of any door that is frequently used by you should be an auspicious direction as given according to your Kua number (see pages 59–60). When practising Flying Star feng shui, however, judgement must be used on whether to use the direction of the main door or direction of the whole house.

3. Superimposing the Lo Shu grid
When locating directions in any home or office, it is necessary to draw the Lo Shu square over the floor plan before you are able to identify the compass directions of each corner of the home. For irregular-shaped homes, the grid is still superimposed onto the home and of course there will then be missing and protruding corners. These corners are analyzed separately.

4. Placement of symbols
When arranging the placement of decorative images that have some auspicious, protective or remedial impact, it is necessary to know the purpose of displaying the image or symbol before deciding where to place it. Remember that in placement, location is generally more important than direction.

5. Space and time dimension
The importance of both these dimensions requires you to make annual investigations to ensure that the spatial feng shui of house and office doors and rooms are not hurt by harmful annual time afflictions.

LEFT City feng shui adapts from the rules of landscape feng shui, thus buildings are seen to be mountains, and roads are viewed as rivers. How one building affects another depends as much on their directional relationships to each other as their shapes, heights and colours.

THE PA KUA METHOD

By now you should be feeling confident enough to start putting your feng shui knowledge into practice. If you are a beginner to feng shui, the Pa Kua method offers a simple way for you to start activating the corners of your home. You can use this easy method to improve your feng shui in any room within your home that you use regularly in order to attract any single one of the eight kinds of luck.

Please note that when you 'feng shui' any room using this method, you will not feel the benefits unless you use the room regularly. It is also a good idea to keep all rooms properly ventilated and allow them to benefit from some sun energy. In the conservatory illustrated here, a feeling of vibrant yang chi is created by the lavish use of plants, light from the sun and the spatial cleanliness and lack of clutter. Anyone using this room could definitely benefit from the application of the Pa Kua method. Placing relevant energizers in each of the corners would greatly enhance the feng shui of this room.

THE PA KUA METHOD

For the Pa Kua method to be effective, you should choose to activate a room that you use often or you will not be able to benefit fully from the enhanced feng shui. The result of enhancing rooms and corners using the element associations of the Pa Kua is often pleasantly surprising.

In applying this particular formula to rooms and apartments, an understanding of the concept of big and small tai chi will be very helpful.

Big tai chi of the whole house

According to Chinese texts, the yin/yang tai chi symbol symbolizes all that makes up the Universe, and so it encapsulates the fullness of heaven, earth and man in all their varying manifestations. In accordance with feng shui theory, the tai chi applies to every microcosm and every macrocosm of space that exists. The big tai chi refers to the larger picture. This can mean seeing the symbol as representing the whole world, or a continent, or a country or a city or a district or a whole house – so bigger or larger is to be viewed in a relative way, and what is big in one context may be small in another. Thus when we describe the bigger tai chi in a feng shui context, we can refer to the tai chi of any space according to how we define the space – so we can refer to the

RIGHT When you superimpose the Pa Kua over the whole floor plan as shown here you will be activating the big tai chi of your home.

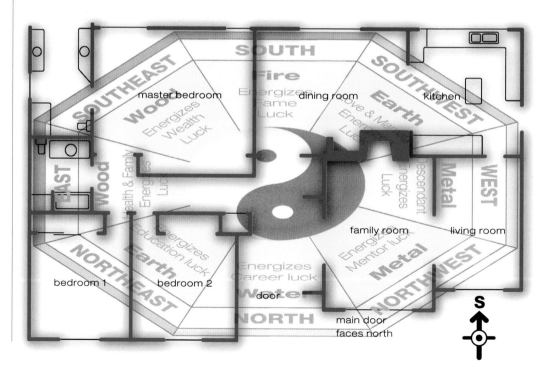

feng shui of the whole house as being the big tai chi. At the same time we can also be referring to the tai chi of an entire office building or an apartment block. Master practitioners of feng shui generally begin by working with the big tai chi to define the parameters of the space they are working with.

The big tai chi means looking at the whole house as a single space entity, and the Pa Kua of eight aspirations is then superimposed onto the floor space of the whole house according to orientations determined with a compass. Implementation of energizers and enhancers must then be undertaken in the light of the big tai chi.

In the example illustrated (left), the door is facing north, so the north side of the Pa Kua is placed where the door is. From the Pa Kua diagram, we know that the wealth luck of this house resides in the master bedroom, while the love and relationship luck is near the kitchen. Career luck is near the entrance door, while mentor luck is in the northwest, which falls in the living room. The layout of this house seems to facilitate the application of feng shui enhancement techniques. Notice the Pa Kua is stretched lengthwise to accommodate the rectangular shape of this house. This is done because the tai chi symbol is not static but flexible, and can be stretched to facilitate application of its many layers of secrets.

Small tai chi of each room

Space can also be manipulated within the confines of separate rooms. This acknowledges that a living abode is made up of several small areas signified by the small tai chi. Thus all living abodes comprise the manifestations of energy as

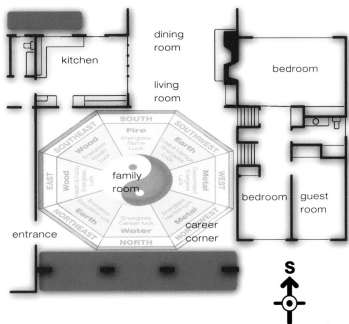

symbolized by the small tai chi. This implies that the Pa Kua of eight aspirations luck can be applied to single rooms.

In the example shown above, the same eight aspirations are superimposed onto the living room of this home. This house has a northeast-facing entrance, so the northeast side of the Pa Kua is placed near the door. It is now possible to identify the career corner of the living room, the wealth area, the love area, the family area and so on, simply by looking at where these sectors are as shown by the Pa Kua. The small tai chi luck of the living room can now be energized using the appropriate elements in each sector.

Use the principles of big and small tai chi to define the space to work with. This is a useful concept to bear in mind, since it holds true for all the compass formulas of feng shui. As an example, you can activate the southwest of your living room or your bedroom to attract love luck if the south-west of your home is missing, or if there is a toilet pressing down on your love luck in the southwest of your house.

ABOVE Here, the Pa Kua showing the corners and what they stand for is placed in a single room. So here you will be able to activate each corner of the room accordingly. This uses the small tai chi concept.

DIVIDING UP SPACE

There are two ways to demarcate space to apply the eight aspirations method of feng shui. This means that to identify the actual corner of the room or home we wish to activate for any one of the eight types of luck, we can use either the pie chart or the Lo Shu grid (a square divided equally into nine smaller, numbered squares) method of demarcation. It is up to you which method you prefer.

Pie Chart method

This method means superimposing the circular compass on to a space and demarcating the space with the chi radiating outwards from the centre. The demarcation of space this way suggests that the distribution of chi comes from the centre point in the room, or the home.

Each sector is shaped like a triangular slice of pie. This method of demarcation is widely used by the Cantonese feng shui masters of Hong Kong. They base their preference for this method on their belief that chi revolves around the compass and that inside any space this is the way chi is to be measured to have meaning. Greater emphasis is thus placed on the 360 degrees of the compass.

Lo Shu grid method

In this method, the compass is used to read the orientation. In addition, the square Lo Shu grid is superimposed over the floor plan to define the parameters of the space that is under investigation or to be activated.

The illustrations here show the difference in the two methods. Both require the compass to define the directions. The difference lies in defining the space that falls into each direction sector. I prefer to use the grid method, as I find it easier to work with a regular square or rectangular shape. You could experiment with each method to see which suits you best.

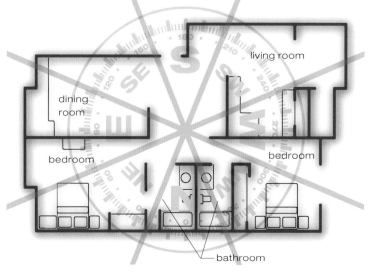

The Pie Chart Method

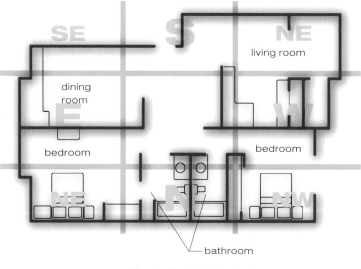

The Lo Shu Grid Method

MAKING HAPPY SPACE

Once you have developed the ability to superimpose the eight aspirations Pa Kua onto the different rooms of your home and also onto your whole house, you have at your fingertips a certain flexibility of application. You can choose which corners and which rooms you want to activate, and concentrate your feng shui efforts on corners and rooms you use the most. You must be the one to make judgements as to where and how you want to activate the big tai chi and where you can more efficiently activate the small tai chi. There are no simple answers to these choices since there are usually localized factors to take into account. Every person is also different with respect to tastes, attitudes and what they want out of life.

Respect your inner voice

In the practice of feng shui, as with everything else, personal creativity, tastes and individual priorities must be acknowledged to obtain maximum results. Do not use anything, paint any colour or place any piece of art or object that you do not like. Respect yourself and your own inner voice. This is the best way to ensure that your personal chi blends with the way you decorate and arrange your rooms. Unless you have a positive interaction with all the objects you place in your home, they will not have as much power to actualize good luck for you. For example, if you really hate the colour pink, then no matter how good this colour may be for attracting love into your life, my advice is not to use it. This is because your dislike is related to your own auric field at some unconscious level.

Also, as we grow older our tastes and aspirations will change. So you can change your tastes as much and as often as you wish, as well as rearrange your rooms, your furniture and the decorative objects you use to activate your corners.

I change my rooms all the time. This creates beneficial movement of chi, and ensures that the chi of my home never gets tired, so my life never stagnates. This reflects my approach to feng shui and also my approach to life. I view life as a dynamic process of new opportunities, new colours and new experiences. Each and every day something new manifests. I never forget that in feng shui there is always an alternative way to go.

To create happy space around you, think of what makes you feel energized, then do the same for your space. Every corner of your home will benefit from attention. When the corners of your rooms are made happy, they will reward you a thousandfold.

ABOVE Creating happy space means using colours, paintings and decorative images you like. Feng shui is a creative practice and you must put something of your own energy into your space for your feng shui to be effective.

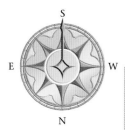

THE SOUTH BRINGS RECOGNITION

The trigram for the south is Li, which means fire – the kind of fire that suggests brightness, intense yang energy and success. South is associated with the horse, the phoenix and the snake – three auspicious symbols that mean fame and recognition. The horse brings speed and endurance that enables you to triumph over competitors. The snake brings skills of diplomacy, while the phoenix brings opportunities that open pathways to new triumphs.

If you activate the bright energy of the south in any part of your home with any of these celestial symbols or with bright lights and objects of a red colour, you will find your success luck magnified. Fame and success, recognition of your capabilities and the popularity of the masses will be some of the luck brought to you.

Those who are in professions whose success is dependent on popularity and public acclaim should ensure that the south sector of their homes is never afflicted by the presence of toilets. Nor should the south corners be 'locked up', thereby creating silent stagnant energy there. Instead it should be open space and always well lit. If possible keep a small red light turned on continuously. Plants in the south also bring good fortune as this evokes the productive cycle of the five elements – wood produces fire.

RIGHT The lamp placed next to the bed in this illustration brings in yang as well as fire energy. In the south corner of the room this will activate recognition luck for the sleeping couple. To make it work, keep the lamp turned on through the night or at least for a minimum of three hours.

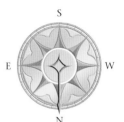

THE NORTH GENERATES CAREER LUCK

The trigram of the north is Kan, which means water. When you use water to activate the north of your whole house, you will see the fast results in the area of your career and your business. So, for example, the placement of an aquarium, or if possible, a Koi pond, in the north is an excellent way of activating great career and business luck.

Activating individual rooms

It is also a good idea to place smaller water features to energize the north sectors of the individual rooms. Thus the north side of the dining room as well as the north side of the living room can be activated with symbols of the water element, such as a painting showing water or an aquarium with live fish. Though some feng shui masters maintain that the placement of fish images or ornaments can signify water, which brings career and business luck, I prefer to use real water for this purpose.

Painting the north wall blue or deep purple (blue stands for water) is also beneficial. Another idea is to paint the north wall white, silver or gold, or place white, silver, or gold curtains and carpets here. In addition, because metal activates the water in the productive cycle (see page 21), you can also use metal energy in these parts of the room. For example, a metallic stereo system placed here would be beneficial. You can be as creative, as daring and as original as you wish.

Just remember that to benefit from your feng shui efforts you must use the rooms that you energize. And any water feature that is created outside the home must face a door or window for its benefits to be felt.

However you should never activate water in the bedroom, since having water here can create losses. In fact, generally, when using the Pa Kua activating method it is a good idea to leave the bedroom alone. The sleeping area is best left non-activated, since too much yang energy could be disruptive. The best rooms to energize are the living room, the dining room and the family room.

ABOVE Painting the north wall of your home blue to represent water is a good activator of feng shui career luck.

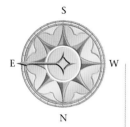

THE EAST BRINGS GOOD HEALTH

The element of the east is wood, and the trigram of this sector is Chen, meaning wood. In feng shui, east is a very important direction because this is the place of the Green Dragon, one of the four celestial animals of the Chinese zodiac and the ultimate symbol of good fortune. This direction is filled with the most sheng chi – also translated as growth chi. Because of this, the east is the ideal part of any home for the sons of the family to have their bedrooms.

BELOW A dragon placed near water or on the east wall of the living room brings great good luck.

Place the image of the dragon on the east wall of the living room. The dragon should hold a symbolic pearl and spout water. I am often asked how many dragons to place here to generate maximum luck for the family, and my reply is always 'as many as you wish, but make sure you have the karma to carry the number of dragons you display'. For example, not everyone is able to sustain the tremendous yang energy of nine dragons. Thus, even when dragons bring much good fortune, it is better not to be too greedy if you cannot sustain them – a single celestial creature is quite sufficient. Or five, at most – unless you were born in the year of the dragon, or you already hold a high position in government or business. Place your dragon image near or inside water – let it be neither too large nor too small.

Activating the east brings good health, longevity and descendants' luck. It also creates the luck that is conducive to the accumulation of wealth assets for the family. Wood element energy grows upward and outward, sending many branches into the sky. The symbolic meaning of this is amazing good fortune if you place the symbols correctly.

Choose from the many decorative objects or, if you prefer natural objects, make free use of plants. Live young plants with broad leaves are excellent for accumulating wealth chi. Alternatively, try and find a 'wealth tree' made of semi-precious stones such as citrine or aventurines (make sure they are genuine and not plastic). Choose an abundant-looking tree with a solid trunk to ensure a firm foundation, and tie on symbolic coins with red or gold ribbon.

S
E — W
N

THE WEST PROTECTS FAMILY LUCK

In traditional feng shui lore, the west has always been identified as the place of the White Tiger, one of the four celestial animals of the Chinese zodiac (the other three are the Green Dragon of the East, the Black Tortoise of the North and the Crimson Phoenix of the South). A strong symbol of protection, the White Tiger is the most ferocious of the four celestial guardians.

In the later heaven arrangement of the trigrams, the west is home to the trigram of joyousness – Tui – also known as the river or lake trigram. Thus the west has been designated as the space where happiness arises as a result of a happy family.

When the chi in the west part of the home is protected and energized, the family stays together and remains healthy and strong. All the older members of the family will live a long life. Both the patriarch and the matriarch, whose luck theoretically resides on both sides of the west (the northwest and southwest respectively), will enjoy increasing happiness and good fortune through the passing years. It is thus vital to keep the chi of the west side of the home moving smoothly and in harmony.

The west belongs to the element of metal and its colour is white. It is not necessary to place the image of the White Tiger since not everyone is able to sustain the 'presence of the tiger' in the home. It is more skilful to activate the element of metal or the element of earth, since earth gives birth to metal under the productive cycle.

The best activators of chi for the west are the vast variety of gold coins that are now coming out of China and Taiwan. There is truly amazing research being carried out in these countries to copy many of the ancient antique coins of the golden ages of past dynasties. I also really like the gold ingots, which are of course such stunning energizers, not just to attract prosperity into the home but also to act as powerful talismans and amulets. Gold or gold colour has powerful wealth-creating energy.

You can, if you like, also look for the powerful swords made with coins, but I am quite happy sticking to my coins, my ingots and my special metal fan and bat amulets. Fans are especially powerful protectors and bats bring the luck of magnificent abundance. In addition, hanging three coins tied with the endless knot (see page 178 for an illustration) is another very strong energizer.

LEFT Coins made of brass or with antique finish are excellent for activating the West sections of the rooms of your home. Gold ingots are equally good.

51

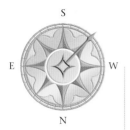

S
E W
N

THE SOUTHWEST IS FOR MARRIAGE

The southwest is the place of Kun, the matriarchal trigram that enhances the luck of relationships, bringing with it the promise of romance, love and the start of

RIGHT Red peonies are said to jazz up one's love life considerably. Placed in the southwest, they attract very good husbands.

a new phase in the lives of people of marriageable age. To the Chinese there are three major happy occasions – hei see – in life. Of the three (a birth, a marriage and a longevity birthday), it is marriage that is generally regarded as the most significant of the double happiness occasions. So the word double happiness has come to symbolize the marriage union, and placing this symbolic image in the southwest makes for a most powerful talisman to create the luck of marriage.

I have seen the powerful effect of the double happiness symbol work wonders with confirmed bachelors! I have also seen the negative effect of a missing southwest corner in the home – this usually manifests as a total absence of marriage prospects for the beautiful daughters and eligible sons of families. In my own home there is no such danger, of course, since the southwest corners of every important room are activated with many different symbols – from mandarin ducks to red peonies (said to attract wonderful husbands for eligible young ladies) to crystal balls and the strategic placement of lights and faceted glass hangings that invite in rainbow rays of sunshine. I also have a beautiful dragon and phoenix image, the other powerful marriage enhancer.

The best way to activate the southwest for the eligible younger generation of the family is to make certain this corner of the home is not afflicted by the presence of a toilet, a store room or the kitchen. To attract good spouses keep the southwest well lit all through the day and night, and make sure the balance of yin and yang is maintained.

THE PA KUA METHOD

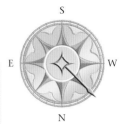

THE NORTHWEST IS FOR MENTORS

The northwest is the place of the patriarch. Here the trigram is Chien – the heaven trigram that signifies the luck of powerful and influential benefactors. If you want help from mentors and support from your bosses, this is the corner to activate. If you want your patriarch to flourish and become prosperous – and this can be your husband or your father – then this too is the corner upon which to focus your feng shui.

The northwest is therefore a very important part of the home. The element of this corner is metal, and in Chinese culture metal also signifies gold. So the northwest is the source of a family's wealth – the kind that is supposed to last through many generations. If you make a wealth vase, and you keep the vase hidden somewhere in the northwest corner of your home, it will benefit the patriarch of the home. If you have a garden and you bury a symbolic wealth box in the northwest of your garden, this too will benefit the patriarch.

There are many different ways to activate the northwest. In essence, it is objects made of metal that are most effective. Ingots and coins are perennial favourites. Cloisonné objects d'art, such as the nine dragon screen illustrated here, are very potent if you like them; also, anything made of or plated in gold. Golden wind chimes are especially auspicious, since the sound of gold is considered to be most beneficial. I activate my northwest with bells and singing bowls made from seven types of metal that include gold and silver to symbolize the energy of the sun and the moon.

BELOW The northwest section of every house should have auspicious images to benefit the patriarch. Screens depicting happy occasions or images of gods and powerful people are helpful.

THE SOUTHEAST BRINGS PROSPERITY

The southeast is the place of the Sun trigram, whose element is wood. It signifies money, not the kind of money referred to in terms of family estate and family net worth, but rather the kind of money associated with income levels. Earnings are a good way to describe the luck of Sun, which is also the movement trigram. Sun indicates activity, which in turn is said to generate income.

If you wish to attract a higher level of regular income, this is the corner to energize. Since this is of the wood element, use plants and flowers to activate this area. In this context, I strongly encourage you to hang fresh flowering plants in the southeast corners indoors as well as in your garden, since this represents excellent feng

shui. This will magnify growth chi for the home. Illustrated here is a conservatory where a profusion of beautiful flowering plants suggest the blossoming of good fortune. When the flowers have stopped blooming, you can get a fresh supply. In these days of instant gardens, you do not need green fingers to harness the blossoming sheng chi of plants. This will help all your plans come to fruition quickly. Remember always to throw away dead plants.

In addition to using plants, you can activate money luck with a small waterfall. Its waters should be kept moving with fish, turtles or pumps to simulate activity. It should be well-landscaped with healthy plants and flowers.

RIGHT This beautiful room would be ideal in the southeast of the home – the profusion of plants signifies an abundance of growth energy symbolizing an expansion of wealth.

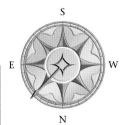

S
E · W
N

THE NORTHEAST FOR EDUCATION LUCK

I have lost count of the number of parents I have advised over the past ten years by sharing with them the powerful Taoist feng shui of the northeast direction. I have known for a long time about how this can be activated to bring excellent examination results, scholastic honours and even scholarships to students.

I taught my daughter Jennifer how to activate her bedroom at school and at university to help her do well in her examinations. Thus, in addition to the Kua formula which helps her select her most auspicious directions to study and to sit facing for her examinations, she also learned to activate the northeast of her rooms to attract scholastic luck. The feng shui helped her to stay very focused, and as a result she has a very impressive academic record.

The way to achieve this is by using a crystal globe. The northeast is an earth element corner. The ruling trigram here is the mountain trigram, so it suggests a time of preparation and also a time of training for the good things that will come later, and energizing this corner with earth energy in the form of crystals can be especially potent.

Crystal power

Crystals are the best and most powerful manifestation of earth energy. Crystals can be natural or manmade. Natural quartz crystals are the best, but the man-made varieties that come from China, carved into a globe, are the most effective for harnessing education luck.

Place the crystal globe, such as the one illustrated on the right, which is about 7.5cm (3in) in diameter, on a table in the Northeast corner of your child's bedroom. You could even use a handmade lead crystal paperweight. Either will activate the chi of education and you should see improvements quite fast.

It is also a good idea to invest in a single-ended natural crystal for your child. This type of crystal is said to be a most efficient way to store energy and knowledge. Let the crystal become a personal study companion amulet for your child. When you get it, first cleanse it of other people's energy by soaking it in a sea- or rock-salt solution for seven days and seven nights. Place it on a table in the northeast when the child is studying and place it underneath the pillow when your child is sleeping. The crystal can be taken into the examination room to bring the luck of education. Keep the crystal wrapped in silk or velvet when not in use.

The dragon carp

Alternatively, you can use the triple fish or the dragon carp image – both of which are just as powerful. The dragon carp symbol is a creature with the tail of a carp and the head of a dragon. It can be ceramic or wood and is usually displayed in pairs. The dragon carp symbolizes the legend of the dragon gate, which is a famous Chinese metaphor.

Crossing the dragon gate is likened to passing the Imperial examinations, and the humble carp transforming into a dragon as it jumps over the dragon gate symbolizes this. Placing the dragon carp in the bedroom is said to manifest scholastic success.

BELOW A crystal globe in the northeast is one of the most potent energizers for those who want education luck. Place it on a table in the northeast of your son or daughter's bedroom.

THE EIGHT MANSIONS FORMULA

The Eight Mansions formula is one of the most powerful of the compass feng shui formulas. Its great merit lies in its easy practicality. Since it deals exclusively with personalized auspicious and inauspicious directions, anyone can use it to great benefit.

The Eight Mansions formula shows you how to find your best and worst directions, and once you know these directions all you need is to invest in a good and reliable compass. From then on it is only a matter of taking some trouble to always check your sitting and facing directions – when you sleep, sit, work and give a presentation, for instance. Making this small effort is all that is needed to get the most out of auspicious directions.

Once you get into the habit of checking your directions, your life will never be the same again. Good feng shui will have changed it forever.

THE EIGHT MANSIONS FORMULA

Feng shui for interior spaces takes on exciting possibilities when we start to use the formula-based natal charts. These represent the compass technology of feng shui – referred to as Eight Mansions.

These charts are truly invaluable for addressing different dimensions of feng shui that take account of the dynamics of changing luck patterns over time. In this and the following chapters I will be introducing you to the use of feng shui charts, which will give your practice of feng shui a quantum leap.

This is an elementary introduction to the scientific aspects of feng shui. It is a little harder to learn, but very much easier to practise since there is less subjectivity. What is required for success is accuracy in taking directions with a proper compass. Accurate directions are required to create the charts. The subjectivity comes in when we have to choose between different options based on what the different charts are telling us about the feng shui of our homes and offices. We have to decide how much weight to place on each of the different formulas and methods.

I hope this will convince those who look upon feng shui as a spiritual esoteric practice. It is not. Remember there is the Western approach to science and there is also the Chinese approach. As we discovered in Chapter 1, there is some mystery to the Chinese view of the Universe in that it focuses on an intangible concept – that of energy, the dragon's cosmic chi – so we should be forgiven if we are tempted to think there are spiritual overtones to feng shui practice.

In introducing you to different feng shui charts I am sharing with you some powerful ways to read the intangible chi of your home space based on very tangible information (compass directions, dates of construction and so forth). It is these tangible facts about a building that enable the feng shui practitioner to draw up the building's various charts, known as natal charts. These charts reveal information about the chi of the different parts of the building, which are expressed as different compass corners. They are excellent for improving the feng shui of your interior spaces and have the potential to effect big changes in your luck.

Eight Mansions charts use the facing direction of the main door (this is the

RIGHT Illustrated here is the Eight Mansions chart of a house facing north. The chart can be analysed to show how each resident's luck is affected according to where his/her room is located.

SE	**S**	**SW**
FU WEI personal growth	**TIEN YI** health	**WU KWEI** five ghosts
NIEN YEN romance	**KUA 4** SITS SOUTH	**LUI SHAR** six killings
CHUEH MING total loss	**SHENG CHI** wealth	**HO HAI** bad luck
NE	**N**	**NW**

(E on left, W on right)

direction you look out to if you are standing inside the front door). In addition to using Eight Mansions charts in this way you can combine them with your Kua number to determine your personalized

Eight Mansions directions. These are described on page 66 and are worked out by first calculating your Kua number as described below. In the charts below the Kua number appears in the central square.

LEFT This is an example of an Eight Mansions chart of a house superimposed onto its interior layout. Note that the Eight Mansions chart of any house defines the luck of the house based on the facing direction of its main door.

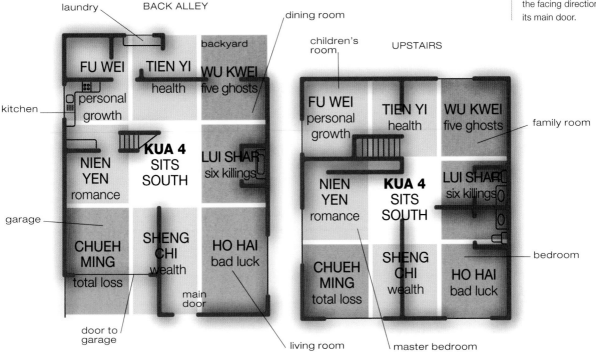

FRONT ROAD

KNOWING YOUR KUA NUMBER

Practising feng shui becomes very meaningful when you arrange rooms and furniture to facilitate the usage of the personalized directions of family members. Knowing the Kua formula of Eight Mansions feng shui is almost mandatory to practising personalized feng shui that brings the fullest benefit to every resident in the home. The Kua formula is probably the fastest working and most user-friendly of all the formulas of feng shui.

To use it, all you need to do is work out your personal Kua number (see page 60) and from there determine your lucky and unlucky directions, as well as your lucky trigram, lucky number and lucky element.

After that it is a question of using this information to create the best feng shui possible from your interior space. Start by learning the formula and determining your directions, then follow through with the tips in this chapter and throughout the book that show you the different ways to use your directions. With practice you should be able to incorporate this formula with other methods and formulas of feng shui to create a powerfully balanced and harmonious chi energy for all your interiors.

The formula differs for men and women. Follow these simple steps:

1 Take your year of birth and convert it to the lunar year. (If you were born in January or early February deduct a year from your year of birth. If you were born in other months, the lunar calendar year is the same as the Western calendar.)

2 Take the last two digits of your year of birth and add them. Keep adding until the sum of the addition is a single digit (for example, if you were born on 4 April 1978, add 7+8=15, then 1+5=6. The next step depends on whether you are male or female.

3 If you are male, deduct from 10, so 10-6=4 and your Kua is 4. If you are calculating for a child born in or after the year 2000, deduct from 9 instead of 10.

4 If you are female, then you add 5, so 5+6=11, then 1+1=2 and your Kua is 2. If you are calculating for a child born in or after the year 2000, add 6 instead of 5.

From the Kua formula, determine your directions and element from the chart below. Start by determining your Kua number and from that look up your different good and bad luck directions paying careful attention to the fine tuning of good and bad luck. Also note your self element and your direction group. The Kua formula reveals many clues for you to personalize your feng shui. This is what makes it such a valuable formula. It is a good idea to learn your personalized feng shui details so that you can enhance your personal feng shui anywhere, anytime.

KUA CHART OF PERSONALIZED DIRECTIONS

| | The four auspicious directions | | | | The four unlucky directions | | | | | |
Kua	Wealth	Health	Love	Growth	Bad luck	Five ghosts	Six killings	Total loss	Group	Self element
1	SE	E	S	N	W	NE	NW	SW	East	Water
2	NE	W	NW	SW	E	SE	S	N	West	Earth
3	S	N	SE	E	SW	NW	NE	W	East	Wood
4	N	S	E	SE	NW	SW	W	NE	East	Wood
5	*	*	*	*	*	*	*	*	West	Earth
6	W	NE	SW	NW	SE	E	N	S	West	Metal
7	NW	SW	NE	W	N	S	SE	E	West	Metal
8	SW	NW	W	NE	S	N	E	SE	West	Earth
9	E	SE	N	S	NE	W	SW	NW	East	Fire

* For Kua 5, it becomes Kua 2 for males and Kua 8 for females.

EAST AND WEST GROUPS

According to the Kua formula, everyone belongs to either the east or the west group. These two groups are in conflict with each other and this means that west group people will suffer if they sit facing or are located in east group directions, and east group people are similarly affected if they face or locate in west group directions.

So the first thing to find out from your Kua number is whether you belong to the east or the west group. You will see from the chart of personalized directions that if your Kua number is 1, 3, 4 or 9 you belong to the east group, and all the east group directions – north, south, east and southeast – are auspicious for you. These are marked in blue on the Pa Kua illustrated here. If your Kua number is 2, 5, 6, 7 or 8 then you belong to the west group and all the west group directions – west, northwest, northeast and southwest – are good for you. These are marked in white in the Pa Kua diagram.

The general rule to observe in your home interiors is to try and sit facing one of your own good directions, and to avoid facing one of your bad directions. Then you should likewise try to sleep with your head pointing to one of your good directions and avoid having your head pointing to one of your unlucky directions.

This easy rule is only the start in your practice of personalized feng shui. Of course, there will be many obstacles to you getting everything perfectly oriented to suit your directions. Invariably, I have discovered that tapping one's best direction is harder than it sounds, simply because there are so many practical difficulties to overcome. You should not get disheartened if you cannot get to use your best directions all the time; and if you already have a room and you simply cannot change your sleeping direction, then all you can really do is to file this information inside your head until you can use it the next time (for example, when you move house), and in the meantime try to use your personalized directions more often – at work, when you are out on a date or at a job interview and so forth. Just remember at all times to which group you belong, and strenuously avoid your four bad luck directions.

EAST GROUP:
south
southeast
east
north

KUA NUMBERS:
1,3,4,9

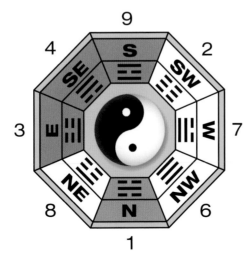

WEST GROUP:
southwest
west
northwest
northeast

KUA NUMBERS:
2,5,6,7,8

LEFT This Pa Kua chart shows which Kua numbers are associated with each compass direction.

THE EIGHT TYPES OF LUCK

The Eight Mansions formula categorizes houses into eight sectors and each sector stands for one type of luck. There are four types of good luck and four types of bad luck. You can use Eight Mansions feng shui to examine whether rooms have good or bad luck, and whether they have the type of luck you want, or need to get rid of.

West group Kua people living in East group Kua houses will find that the distribution of luck in the house will directly clash with their personal good and bad luck directions.

According to master practitioners of the Eight Mansions formula, if you are either the father or the mother of the house, ideally the room you occupy should bring you good luck under both the house chart and under your personal Kua number. If you are one of the children or relatives, it is advisable to use your personal Kua number to select the rooms that are best for you and to ignore the house Eight Mansions chart.

RIGHT This foyer area in front of the main door is very important in feng shui. It must harmonize with your personal sheng chi if the house is to bring you luck.

GOOD LUCK LOCATIONS

Sheng Chi

This signifies the place of wealth and prosperity luck. It is always the entrance to the building and corresponds to the facing direction 'palace' in Flying Star feng shui. This part of the house brings prosperity to the household and its residents, so keep it well activated – no clutter and always a lot of light, space and enhancers.

Nien Yen

This signifies the place of good luck for marriage and romantic luck, and for descendants' luck. This place will be different depending on the facing direction of the house. The charts will reveal the room that has this luck.

Tien Yi

This pinpoints the room with the best health luck. Members of the family more prone to illnesses should be given rooms with tien yi luck.

Fu Wei

This signifies the space with personal development luck. School-age children would benefit from this part of the house.

BAD LUCK LOCATIONS

Ho Hai

This signifies a place of mild bad luck. If you occupy a ho hai room you will find minor irritations annoying you. Projects take longer to come to fruition. There are setbacks and disappointments.

Wu Kwei

This signifies relationship problems and bad luck associated with troublemakers and being a victim of gossip and scandalmongering. Five Ghosts bad luck can sometimes get transformed into immense good luck by the auspicious feng shui charts using other systems and formulas such as Flying Star.

Lui Shar

This signifies six types of misfortunes. The bad luck here can be described as quite severe and it comes in battalions. Illness, loss, death, loss of good name, loss of wealth, loss of descendants – misfortunes in many different manifestations occur.

Chueh Ming

This signifies a state of total loss and usually this can mean bankruptcy or even a whole family being wiped out altogether. In any home, it is a good idea never to stay in a room afflicted by cheuh ming unless the Flying Star chart indicates a change of luck there.

EIGHT MANSIONS CHARTS

The Eight Mansions charts are simply a visually efficient way of showing you how the eight types of luck are distributed in your home. It is called Eight Mansions because there are eight types of 'mansions' with different distributions of chi, and thus different distributions of luck within the house.

Eight Mansions charts use descriptions to reveal the type of chi present. This is different from the trigram charts (see pages 68–70) and Flying Star charts (see pages 88–89) which express information as numbers. All three use the nine squares (known as the Nine Palaces) to express the distribution of chi and all three are based on house orientations, that is on the facing or sitting directions of the house.

On the page opposite you will find the eight Eight Mansions charts. Locate the chart that applies to your house by using a compass to check your house-facing direction, and find the chart that corresponds to that direction. Then use the charts to analyze the Eight Mansions chi distribution within your home. It is really that simple.

Compatibility of house and individual

The Eight Mansions chart describes the distribution of luck in exactly the same way as Eight Mansions works for individuals. When the chi distribution of your home exactly matches your personal good luck and bad luck directions based on your Kua number, then you and the house are said to be compatible and the house is excellent for you. Always try to live in a house that is compatible with your Kua number.

For example, if your Kua number is 1, then your sheng chi direction is southeast. A house facing southeast would be best for you, since the distribution of luck in this house will correspond exactly to what is good for you. In this instance, it is east group people who would find the house to be compatible, since the good and bad luck directions would be the same for the house and for the individual.

RIGHT You can use your feng shui personal directions in a variety of situations. When making a speech, for example, you will be helped if you face the wealth direction based on your Kua number.

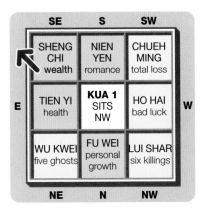

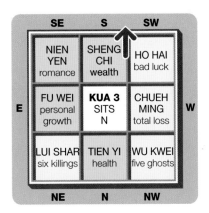

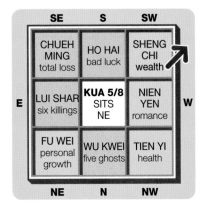

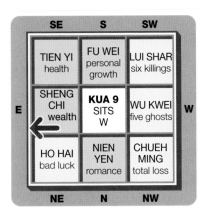

The arrows in the charts indicate the house direction. Note the four good directions (wealth, health, romance and personal growth) and the four unlucky directions (bad luck, five ghosts, six killings and total loss). Identify your lucky and unlucky rooms.

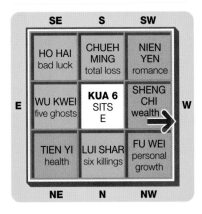

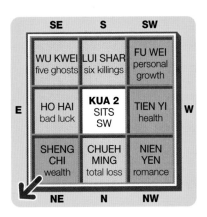

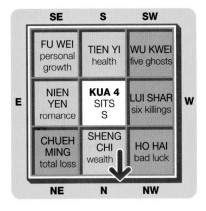

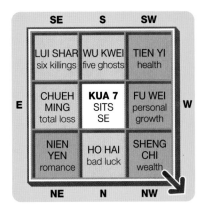

THE HOUSE TRIGRAM FORMULA

The House Trigram formula is a popular branch of the Flying Star set of formulas. It is really a very simple version of Flying Star feng shui and its usefulness is in the way it categorizes houses into eight types. Each of these houses is named after one of the eight trigrams based on the house's sitting direction.

Since each trigram has a corresponding number, we can use this number to create a Lo Shu chart that sets out the energy of each of the nine sectors of the home. Each of these sector's energy is defined as a number. The annual numbers are then added into the trigram chart. Reading the two numbers of each little grid – the trigram number and the annual number – gives us a very accurate reading of the chi energy of each of the sectors.

The way to practise this method is to study the numbers that affect your bedroom and your main door. This will enable you to place 'cures' in any afflicted parts of the house. These cures will work for one year only.

THE HOUSE TRIGRAM FORMULA

Especially helpful in analyzing the annual and monthly luck of different parts of the home, this formula can be used on its own or combined with annual numbers for a fuller analysis.

To apply the House Trigram formula, the trigram of a house must first be determined. Look at the eight trigrams of the feng shui Pa Kua based on the later heaven arrangement, shown below. Each trigram is allotted a direction according to the sequence of trigrams shown in the Pa Kua. Note the names of the trigrams. Then note the corresponding Lo Shu numbers, which are given in the list opposite. Unlike the Eight Mansions formula, which is based on the facing direction of a house, the trigram charts are based on its sitting direction (see page 28).

When your house is sitting in the:

North – it is a **KAN** house (**1**)
South – it is a **LI** house (**9**)
East – it is a **CHEN** house (**3**)
West – it is a **TUI** house (**7**)
Southeast – it is a **SUN** house (**4**)
Southwest – it is a **KUN** house (**2**)
Northeast – it is a **KEN** house (**8**)
Northwest – it is a **CHIEN** house (**6**)

From the reigning Lo Shu number, the chart can be generated based on the flight sequence (see page 30).

RIGHT This shows a Li south-sitting house. This sitting direction of a house or building determines its Trigram chart. First get the facing direction. The exact opposite of that is the sitting direction.

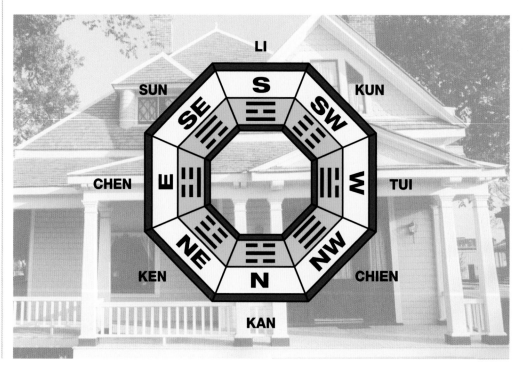

THE TRIGRAM CHARTS

Now you have established the ruling trigram and the Lo Shu number of your house, you can use the trigram charts. The charts are read by superimposing them onto the house floor plan and then analyzing the meanings of the single numbers in the different sectors. After that, another number is added to each of the sections (see page 70) to give you even more information. These are known as annual flying star numbers and are not to be confused with the mountain and water flying star numbers, which are shown on pages 88–89.

Below are the eight charts of the trigram houses. You can see by now how important and significant the Lo Shu chart is in the use of compass formula feng shui.

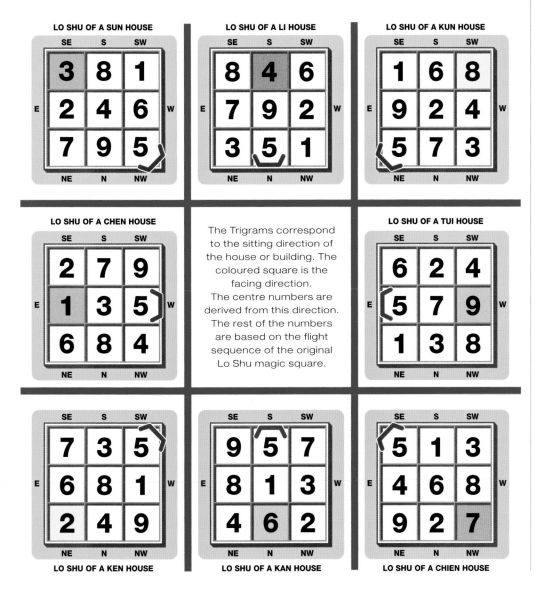

LO SHU OF A SUN HOUSE

SE	S	SW
3	8	1
2	4	6
7	9	5

E — W · NE N NW

LO SHU OF A LI HOUSE

SE	S	SW
8	4	6
7	9	2
3	5	1

E — W · NE N NW

LO SHU OF A KUN HOUSE

SE	S	SW
1	6	8
9	2	4
5	7	3

E — W · NE N NW

LO SHU OF A CHEN HOUSE

SE	S	SW
2	7	9
1	3	5
6	8	4

E — W · NE N NW

The Trigrams correspond to the sitting direction of the house or building. The coloured square is the facing direction.
The centre numbers are derived from this direction. The rest of the numbers are based on the flight sequence of the original Lo Shu magic square.

LO SHU OF A TUI HOUSE

SE	S	SW
6	2	4
5	7	9
1	3	8

E — W · NE N NW

SE	S	SW
7	3	5
6	8	1
2	4	9

E — W · NE N NW
LO SHU OF A KEN HOUSE

SE	S	SW
9	5	7
8	1	3
4	6	2

E — W · NE N NW
LO SHU OF A KAN HOUSE

SE	S	SW
5	1	3
4	6	8
9	2	7

E — W · NE N NW
LO SHU OF A CHIEN HOUSE

COMBINED TRIGRAM AND ANNUAL CHARTS

The charts on this page show how each trigram chart can be combined with the annual Flying Star numbers for 2003 and 2004. Using these charts in conjunction with the meanings of the numbers on the following pages will open up countless opportunities for you to improve your feng shui, and to remedy the afflictions of your rooms from year to year. As you learn to combine the numbers, you will develop the expertise needed to combine with 2005 numbers and beyond.

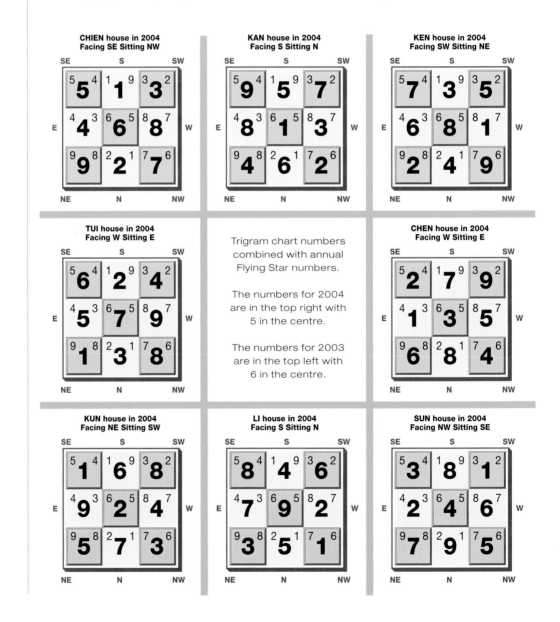

Trigram chart numbers combined with annual Flying Star numbers.

The numbers for 2004 are in the top right with 5 in the centre.

The numbers for 2003 are in the top left with 6 in the centre.

READING THE TRIGRAM CHART

Another important concept to understand is the cycles of time, known as Periods (see page 85), that affect the meaning of the annual numbers. Every 20 years the period changes. Period Seven ends on 4 February 2004 and Period Eight begins. This is important when it comes to using the tables of meanings on pages 72–80, where the Periods are sometimes referred to. In different periods, numbers have different luck meanings. So a room that is lucky one year, may need bad luck remedies the next year.

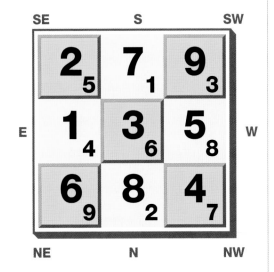

LEFT The little numbers in the Chen chart are 2003 numbers. Now try filling in the year 2004 numbers which have the 5 in the centre and see how the luck of the sectors change from one year to the next.

Start with the central number

The example on this page is a Chen house, because it is sitting east and facing west. Since the number of east is 3, this becomes the centre number of the chart. With the centre number in place, the rest of the numbers can be filled in according to the flight sequence (see page 30) of the numbers found in the Lo Shu chart.

Fill in the smaller numbers

The smaller numbers in each sector are the annual numbers for the year 2003. Put the appropriate annual number in each sector to create a chart showing the two numbers in each square (the annual numbers for the next 20 years are given on page 36).

Using the chart

Now superimpose the chart over the floor plan of your house. This chart reveals the map luck of the house, enabling you to identify which sector has good or bad luck during any particular year. The luck of each sector is read in accordance with the meanings associated with the combination of the two numbers, given in the trigram charts on the following pages. To interpret the meanings of the number combinations, you will need to know about the element interactions of the numbers as well as the meanings of the numbers themselves. Knowing how to read this chart thus reveals important information for residents in the different sectors of the house. It is not difficult to learn this system of feng shui. All that is needed is a basic knowledge of the Lo Shu square, the flight sequence of its numbers and the numbers that are associated with each of the eight directions.

Chart analysis

The trigram tables set out the meanings of the combination of the trigram with the annual number (see page 70). They will enable you analyze of each of the eight houses in years 2003 and 2004, shown opposite. The tables summarize the key meanings of the numbers, and will assist you in the practice of feng shui.

UNDERSTANDING TRIGRAM CHARTS – NUMBER 1 AND ANNUAL NUMBERS

The number 1 is a white number and is regarded as one of the three luckiest numbers in this method of feng shui analysis. If your bedroom is located in a sector of the house that has the number 1, it is a lucky indication. When combined with 1, 6 or 8 the luck is further magnified.

Trigram number	Annual number	Meanings	Enhancers/Remedies
1	1	Excellent for academic studies, research and creative work. Good money luck. If afflicted by monthly star 5 or 2, there could be kidney-related illness. Accidents can also happen, caused by excessive drinking and alcoholic problems as this signifies excessive water. A double 1 is, however, a very good indication.	To enhance and also to control affliction, use a six-rod all-metal wind chime. Watch out for when the 5 or 2 flies in during specific months. To be safe, hang metal wind chimes here.
1	2	There could be marriage problems and also a danger of losing a child through miscarriage. Beware of car accidents. The number 2 is not a good number to combine with 1 – it makes it afflicted.	Use plants to exhaust the water number 1 and strengthen the earth element.
1	3	Heartache is caused by gossip and slandering. There could be lawsuits and legal entanglements brought by the 3.	Use water to enhance and water plants to transform the hostility of 3.
1	4	Political luck. Media and publicity luck. Romance luck, especially for women. Good writing luck for authors. This is a very good combination for literary work.	Use slow-moving water, but not too much, as this could bring problems associated with sex.
1	5	Health problems; sickness, food poisonings. Injury caused by accidents. The 5 is always to be feared.	Use a six-rod metal wind chime to exhaust the 5. This also strengthens the 1 of water.
1	6	Excellent career luck. Promotion. Good money luck. Headaches, especially when the monthly 5 or 2 enters.	Enhance with still metal such as coins, ingots and gold art.
1	7	Good money luck in period 7, but it is also an indication that there will be cut-throat competition. Bad in period 8.	Enhance with crystals or a gem tree – look for citrines as these interact well with 1.
1	8	Excellent wealth luck. There could be misunderstandings between loved ones, siblings and good friends. Business partners have problems.	Enhance with white crystals, and also with moving water to attract wealth luck.
1	9	Good for both career and money luck, but can turn bad when 5 flies in. Eye problems.	No need to enhance. Go easy with reds.

UNDERSTANDING TRIGRAM CHARTS – NUMBER 2 AND ANNUAL NUMBERS

The number 2 is the illness number and it is regarded as one of the danger numbers in this method of feng shui analysis. If your bedroom is located in a sector of the house that has the number 2, you should install wind chime remedies immediately, especially when the annual 2 and monthly 2 flies in to strengthen the illness luck.

Trigram number	Annual number	Meanings	Enhancers/Remedies
2	1	Stress develops in the marriage if this combination is in the bedroom. There is danger of miscarriage and other accidents – and loss of loved one.	Use metal wind chimes to control and exhaust the bad star 2. It is also a good idea to move to another room.
2	2	Not a good indication. Magnifies strong negative feelings. Illness and accidents possible. The double 2 is to be feared.	Six-rod wind chimes, coins and bells. What is needed is strong metallic sounds.
2	3	Arguments and misunderstandings of the most severe kind. There is hostility, back-stabbing, hatred and legal disputes. If your room is afflicted with the 2/3 combination it can be a stressful time.	Use still (yin) water to cool tempers. Do not disturb the energy here with chimes, music or noise. Keep the room very quiet.
2	4	Wives and mothers-in-law quarrel and fight. Family disharmony is in the air. Good indications for writers and those in the journalism field. Good for those at school but the luck can be short-lived.	Use still (yin) water in an urn to create some harmony. Also try using smooth crystal balls. This can be quite effective to overcome in-law problems.
2	5	Extremely inauspicious. Total loss and catastrophe. This is one of the most dangerous combinations in Flying Star technique, and when the 5 flies in, anyone staying here can suddenly develop terminal illness.	Use strong wind chimes. Beware – do not have fire or there could be a death. Whenever the 2 and the 5 occur together it is necessary to be careful.
2	6	Very easy life of ease and leisure, power and authority. This auspicious combination is spoilt if a five-rod wind chime is placed here – the trinity (tien ti ren) gets activated in a negative way.	Do not use wind chimes. If there is sickness related to the stomach, place a red amulet here. Placing a crystal gem tree here would be excellent.
2	7	There is money during Period Seven but luck of children will not be good. Problems conceiving children. Unscrupulous people at work will tend to politic against you.	Use metal bells and metal wind chimes. Hang a sword of coins to overcome work aggravations. Also use a porcelain rooster.
2	8	Richness and wealth, but there is ill health, although this can be remedied.	Use water to overcome bad health star and the symbol of good health, the wu lou.
2	9	Extremely bad luck. Nothing succeeds unless remedied. Not a good indication for children.	Use water plants. Also use coins or wind chimes.

UNDERSTANDING TRIGRAM CHARTS – NUMBER 3 AND ANNUAL NUMBERS

The number 3 is the quarrelsome number in this and Flying Star feng shui. If this number afflicts your room, you will have to endure hostility and quarrelsome luck unless you install the necessary remedies.

Trigram number	Annual number	Meanings	Enhancers/Remedies
3	1	Heartache caused by gossip and slandering. There could be lawsuits and legal entanglements.	Use water to enhance and water plants. If already engaged in a lawsuit, move temporarily to a less afflicted room. An obelisk natural crystal will help.
3	2	Dangerous for those in politics; lawsuits, even jail. Gossip, slander. Bad luck for women; obesity.	Some Masters recommend gold and fire. I also like using paintings that feature goldfish in gold and red.
3	3	Gossip and slander. Quarrels. Robbery. A very dangerous indication that can get out of hand very easily. You must make every effort not to have too much noise in the part of the house afflicted by the double 3. In Flying Star feng shui, the double 3 brings hostility and aggravations.	Use a sword of coins – metal is needed but not the sounds. Still water is always helpful, so blue carpets and curtains can help to soften the situation. Use dark rather than light blue.
3	4	Heartache caused by sexual scandal. This manifests in the presence of third parties into your family life. You can overcome this with crystal under the bed.	Use bright lights to dissipate scandalous chi – also place an amethyst crystal under the bed where the feet are.
3	5	Loss of wealth. Severe cash-flow problems. If your bedroom is here, financial loss is severe. If the kitchen is here, sickness is inevitable.	Exhaust the 5 with a copper mountain painting. Yin metal is very effective to overcome affliction.
3	6	Time of slow growth. Leg injuries. Bad for young males.	Use still (yin) water.
3	7	You will get robbed or burgled. Violence. Possibility of injury from knives or guns. Blood.	Use still (yin) water. This will exhaust the ferocity of 7 in this combination.
3	8	Not good for children under 12 years. Danger to limbs.	Use bright lights to cure.
3	9	Robbery encounter. Lawsuits. Fights.	Use still (yin) water.

UNDERSTANDING TRIGRAM CHARTS –
NUMBER 4 AND ANNUAL NUMBERS

The number 4 in Flying Star and House Trigram feng shui is considered an auspicious number as it brings academic luck. It is also regarded as the romance number although this can turn scandalous when it meets up with excessive water energy.

Trigram number	Annual number	Meanings	Enhancers/Remedies
4	1	Very good romance luck but too much water leads to sex scandals. Affairs lead to unhappiness and break up of family. Must guard against being carried away. But excellent creative and writing luck.	A Kuan Yin statue or an image of a laughing Buddha for some divine help might enhance the luck further and also save you from going overboard.
4	2	Illness of internal organs. Husband has extramarital affair, or at least could be lured into a situation of some risk – could lead to scandals.	Use an amethyst crystal under the bed. Do this as a precaution – make certain the amethyst used is big enough (10–14cm/4–6in).
4	3	Emotional stress because of relationship, and sexual and emotional problems.	Use a strong red to overcome – perhaps cinnamon-red cushions, curtains and wall hangings.
4	4	Excellent for writing and creative luck. Very attractive to opposite sex. Romance will flourish.	Fresh flowers to enhance growth of romance. Be wary of having too much water, but activate with the double happiness and other symbols of romance.
4	5	Sexually transmitted skin diseases. Breast cancer. The illness risk is great.	Use a painting of water and a mountain as a cure. Also use a wind chime to control the 5.
4	6	Money luck but creativity dries up. Bad luck indicated for women, especially pregnant women, who should move to another room.	Strengthen earth element with crystals. Also place the symbol of health, known as a wu lou, by the bedside.
4	7	Bad luck in love. Will get cheated by the opposite sex. Sickness of the thighs and lower abdomen. If in the bedroom, the affliction is severe. If the front door is in this sector, place a pair of Chi Lin here.	Use yang water to control. There are several water cures you can consider for this, but if in the bedroom use blue or black.
4	8	Excellent career luck for writers. Bad for very young children. Injury to limbs indicated.	Use lights to combat the threat to children. Enhance the 8 luck with round, natural crystals – the larger the better.
4	9	A time for preparation. Good for students. Need to be careful of fire breaking out.	Use wood or plants, but make certain fire element does not get too strong.

UNDERSTANDING TRIGRAM CHARTS – NUMBER 5 AND ANNUAL NUMBERS

The number 5 is a very unlucky and dangerous number in this system of feng shui. Each time it flies into your bedroom, or afflicts the main door, it brings illness, accidents and severe financial loss in its wake. Fortunately, it is not too difficult to control.

Trigram number	Annual number	Meanings	Enhancers/Remedies
5	1	Hearing problems and also sex-related illness could break out. The 5 combined with 1 is bad news.	Use six-rod all metal hollow wind chimes. This exhausts the 5 and strengthens the 1.
5	2	Misfortunes and extreme bad luck. Illness may be fatal – it is a good idea to move out of the afflicted room. These two numbers together are to be feared. Illness is certain, but losses can also result.	Use plenty of six-rod wind chimes, gold coins and metal energy because the combination of 2 with 5 is self-sustaining and the effect is very severe.
5	3	Money troubles. Disputes. Bad business luck – could lead to lawsuits that trigger extreme stress to the residents.	Use six coins stuck onto walls and placed above doorway.
5	4	Creativity dries up. Sickness. Skin problems could become severe.	Use water/mountain. Place plants with large leaves to absorb the bad energy and to enhance the 4. Do not use plants with thin spiky leaves.
5	5	A very critical combination. Extreme danger indicated by the double 5 – mishaps take place with great ferocity. Serious illness and accidents that can be fatal. Take care.	Use metal 6-rod wind chimes to overcome. Paint the room white and also have 6 gold coins under the carpet and over the doorway.
5	6	Bad luck for finances. Loss. Diseases related to the head region. Danger also to the man.	Place 6 coins under the carpet in the room to help strengthen the metal energy.
5	7	Arguments abound. Mouth-related illness.	Coins and bells are a good remedy here – also wind chimes will be a great help. But in Period Eight this combination becomes dangerous.
5	8	Problems related to the limbs, joints and bones. It is necessary to be careful of rough sports.	Use yang water to pacify.
5	9	Bad luck all round. Do not speculate or gamble as you are sure to lose. Eye problems. Danger of fire.	Use water and also red and gold paintings. Wind chimes are also effective against the 5/9 combination.

UNDERSTANDING TRIGRAM CHARTS – NUMBER 6 AND ANNUAL NUMBERS

The number 6 is another lucky white number and is regarded as one of the three luckiest numbers in Flying Star and Trigram feng shui analysis. If your bedroom is located in a sector of the house that has the number 6, it indicates extremely good fortune.

Trigram number	Annual number	Meanings	Enhancers/Remedies
6	1	Financial luck and high achievers in the family manifest joyousness. It is an excellent indication of good fortune. Headaches through excessive stress.	Enhance with metal energy as metal creates water and also enhances the 6. Use a bowl of gold ingots.
6	2	Great affluence and everything successful. Stomach problems. Patriarch could have sickness.	No need to enhance, but control with bells – the idea is to strengthen the 6 while suppressing the 2, so place metallic energy.
6	3	Unexpected windfall. Speculative luck. Leg injury.	Enhance with gemstones, or a bowl of 'diamonds' (Austrian crystals). This is simply the best enhancer of wealth luck. Protect against leg injury with strong plant energy and by removing metal.
6	4	Unexpected windfall for women of the family. Lower body injury. Pregnant women must be careful.	Enhance with smooth and round crystal balls. Do not enhance with metal energy as this could become dangerous.
6	5	Money luck blocked. Sickness could prevail.	Use bells and brass mirrors to overcome the 5 annual.
6	6	Excellent money luck from heaven, but too much metal can be dangerous, so do not enhance with metal.	No need to enhance – better not to.
6	7	Competitive squabbling over money. Arguments. Hostility could break out into something ugly. Also success breeds jealousy. Must tread carefully.	Use water to curb and control the arising of gossip and envy.
6	8	Wealth, popularity, prosperity. Great richness. Probably the best combination in Flying Star technique. Those in love are in for a lonely period.	Enhance with water and make sure you have an entrance or window in that sector – this is a very auspicious combination – use crystal diamonds.
6	9	Money luck. Frustration between generations, leading to arguments between young and old.	Water to reduce the daily friction. Also use a brass mirror to absorb bad chi and reduce the possibility of misunderstandings escalating into something more serious.

UNDERSTANDING TRIGRAM CHARTS – NUMBER 7 AND ANNUAL NUMBERS

The number 7 is lucky in this period, and has brought great prosperity in the years since 1984; but its energy is now fast waning and turning unlucky. By 4 February 2004, the number 7 will have become extremely unlucky and weak, bringing burglary and even accidents and violence leading to serious injury caused by metal. Safeguards must be made to deal with the change of period that is coming.

Trigram number	Annual number	Meanings	Enhancers/Remedies
7	1	Extremely good prosperity luck. But competition is deadly and can turn ugly. Tread carefully with partners and business associates.	Use water feature to strengthen the 1 as this will bring good chi into the combination.
7	2	Money luck dissipates. Children luck is dimmed. Young children should be careful.	Use wind chimes.
7	3	Grave danger of injury to limbs. Be careful. Do not strengthen the metal energy as it will turn dangerous.	Use still (yin) water to overcome and exhaust the metal energy. The water must be in an urn that is at least 45cm (18in) deep.
7	4	Taken for a ride by someone of the opposite sex (use an amulet to guard against losing your money here). Pregnant women should also take care.	Use water. If the home belongs to older people it is necessary to remove flowers from the bedroom.
7	5	Problems caused by excessive gossiping. Danger of poisoning or anything to do with the mouth.	Use metal coins, bells or wind chimes. Also red energy might help in this combination.
7	6	Grave misfortune, although in certain circumstances the auspicious 6 can prevail.	Use water to exhaust the 7.
7	7	Prevalence over competition. Money luck. Sex life gets a boost for young people. Beware of over-indulgence.	Use water to curb excesses. The 7 must be kept under control at all times.
7	8	Same as above but better because of the 8 energy. Here good luck is stronger than the bad luck.	Use water and also lots of crystal energy. This will boost the energy of the 8, bringing good fortune and lots of luck.
7	9	All troubles are caused through vulnerability to sexual advances. There is danger of fire hazards.	Use earth (big boulders) to press down bad luck. The 7 must be kept under control here. Use water chi – blues, blacks and water motifs.

UNDERSTANDING TRIGRAM CHARTS – NUMBER 8 AND ANNUAL NUMBERS

The number 8 is the third white number and is regarded as the luckiest number in House Trigram and Flying Star feng shui. Whenever 8 is present it brings very powerful and strong good fortune energy.

As well as being an intrinsically lucky number, its presence in any of your charts is sure to bring prosperity when it becomes the reigning number of the 20-year period beginning on 4 February 2004.

Trigram number	Annual number	Meanings	Enhancers/Remedies
8	1	Excellent and auspicious prosperity luck. Career advancement. Money luck. But sibling rivalry prevails.	Enhance with water and with crystals. Place ships, or sailing boats filled with 'diamonds', as a powerful enhancer of wealth.
8	2	Wealth creation possible. Properties and asset accumulation. But there is the danger of illness. Generally, however, the 8 is a strong lucky number and will prevail.	Use a mountain picture. A boulder with thick red thread tied round will activate the earth chi. Overcome the 2 with metal energy and enhance the 8 with earth energy.
8	3	Move children away from this sector. Injury to limbs. Some hostility and misunderstanding arising from envy.	Use red or yellow.
8	4	Overpowering matriarch. Love life of younger generation suffers from mother and potential mother-in-law problems. Injury to limbs (protect with an amulet).	Use fire, or red to overcome. Red is especially powerful as this appeases the matriarchal energy.
8	5	Problems related to the limbs, joints and bones of the body. It is necessary to be careful of rough sports, climbing mountains, skiing and other activities using the limbs.	Use water to pacify. Also overcome the threat and danger of accidents by placing a brass mirror in the room.
8	6	Wealth, popularity, prosperity. Great richness. Love life goes through a rough patch but will be smooth in the end.	Enhance with crystals. Make sure there is an entrance or window in that sector to bring in the good luck.
8	7	Prevalence over competition. Money luck. Sex life gets a boost for young people. Beware of over-indulgence.	Use water to curb excesses.
8	8	Excellent wealth creation luck. Very favourable.	No need to enhance.
8	9	Excellent for money and celebration. But misunderstandings between the younger and older generation can turn nasty.	Use water to calm the fire.

UNDERSTANDING TRIGRAM CHARTS – NUMBER 9 AND ANNUAL NUMBERS

The number 9 is the ultimate magnifying number – combining the fullness of heaven and earth. It can be excellent when triggered by an auspicious annual number but it can also be deadly when combined with a 5 or a 2. The main thing about 9 is its strong fire energy. When under control it is excellent but when out of control the 9 can bring disasters.

Trigram number	Annual number	Meanings	Enhancers/Remedies
9	1	Good for both career and money luck, but can turn bad when 5 flies in. Danger of eye problems.	Do not enhance.
9	2	Extremely bad luck. Nothing succeeds unless remedied. Not a good indication for children. Here the 9 magnifies the bad star number 2.	Use water plants. Also use coins or wind chimes. Do not use bright lights here.
9	3	Robbery encounter. Lawsuits. Fights. Fire hazard.	Use still (yin) water.
9	4	A time for preparation. Good for students. Be careful of fire – as a combination, 9/4 possesses hidden dangers, so it is a good idea to be very careful.	Use wood or plants but do not overdo the energizing of fire energy. It is better to have young wood than old wood energy, so young plants will be good here.
9	5	Bad luck all round. Do not speculate or gamble as you are sure to lose. Eye problems. Danger of fire.	Use wind chimes to overcome this potentially deadly combination.
9	6	Money luck. Frustration between generations, leading to arguments between young and old; usually manifest as problems between daughter and father.	Water will reduce the frictions but a better remedy is for any young girl staying in such a room to move to another room.
9	7	Troubles caused through vulnerability to sexual advances. There is also danger of fire hazards.	Use earth (big boulders) to press down bad luck. Also, keep an amulet to ward off danger of being sexually assaulted.
9	8	Excellent for money and celebrations. But misunderstandings between the younger and older generation can turn nasty. There is also danger of envy and insecurities clashing badly.	Use water to calm the fire. Place a large urn of still (yin) water. Fire energy must be pressed down, especially if this occurs in the South.
9	9	Good or bad, depending on other indications. Generally a double 9 can be neutral and depends on the monthly star numbers flying in. When incoming month stars are good, the luck gets magnified. When the incoming month star is 5 or 2, misfortunes are more severe.	Do not enhance.

INTERPRETING A TRIGRAM CHART

To use the trigram charts, superimpose the chart onto the floor plan so that the compass locations of the number combinations are placed on the plan. In the example illustrated here, we have a Chen house, which is sitting east and facing west. Since the number of east is 3, the big centre number in the chart is 3 and from this number the whole chart is created.

Next, look at the numbers for 2003 (shown in the bottom left of each square) and 2004 (shown in the bottom right of each square) to read the luck of the main rooms of this house for these years. The most important parts of the home are its main entrance area and the bedrooms. These have been highlighted in yellow. Look first at the master bedroom and all the bedrooms, and from the annual numbers we can see that residents enjoy good luck in 2003, but in 2004 the good fortune luck begins to dissipate. This becomes clearer when we look at the

entrance area. In 2003 the west sector has the powerfully auspicious 8 but in 2004 the annual number here changes to 7, which has by 2004 turned ugly and dangerous.

Thus you can see that by simply comparing the annual numbers from year to year it is possible to be forewarned of difficult times ahead. Note that the evil star number 7 can be controlled by placing water in that part of the house. This is because water exhausts the metal element chi of 7.

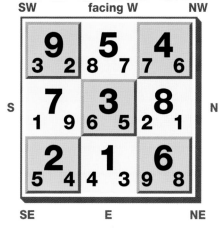

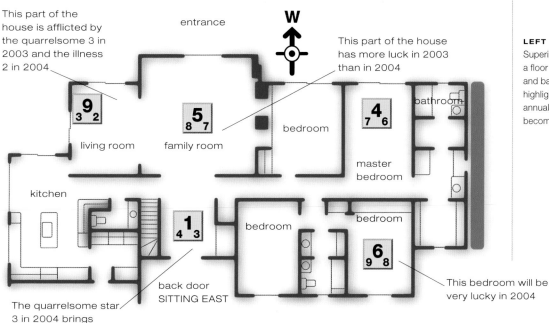

LEFT AND ABOVE Superimposed over a floor plan, the good and bad luck areas highlighted by the annual stars will become clear.

81

THE FLYING STAR FORMULA

Not many people realize that feng shui has a time dimension that can be investigated using highly detailed Flying Star annual and monthly charts. Flying Star feng shui is a branch of compass formula feng shui, using the facing direction of buildings, including houses, to determine natal charts that reveal the map luck of those buildings over 20-year periods.

The Flying Star charts offer a map for capturing wealth, relationship and health luck by working on the rooms in the house to benefit residents directly. This is done by identifying and then activating the auspicious mountain and water stars of the chart wherever they occur in the house.

Remember that while space and direction stays constant, time changes and each new cycle of time brings new energy influences that affect health, wealth, finances, romance, marriage, family and personal growth. This is the exciting promise of Flying Star feng shui. If you know how to use it, your life will be forever brightened.

THE FLYING STAR FORMULA

Flying Star natal charts are sometimes referred to as Nine Palaces charts. These charts map out the 'luck' of yang buildings – revealing lucky and unlucky areas via the numbers that get placed in each of the nine sections. These are known as the Nine Palaces of the home.

BELOW As the next period, Period Eight starts on 4 February 2004 and it affects everyone's house. It is recommended by feng shui masters to change your house into a Period Eight house. If possible, it is advised to have at least part of the roof replaced.

The system is known as Flying Star feng shui because the numbers themselves are known as stars, and the numbers move in accordance with compass directions and time periods, so they are called Flying Stars. Feng shui practitioners tend to disagree on various aspects of Flying Star feng shui, so it is useful to be aware of the following:

■ Not all experts are in agreement as to what constitutes the period of a building (see opposite). Some say it is when a building is completely built. Others say it is when the building is last renovated and they also cannot agree on the precise definition of the word renovation. Other practitioners stubbornly maintain it is when the last residents moved in. The house period is a vital issue, since this is the basis of the natal chart.

■ Not all experts are in agreement on how one should determine the facing direction of any building. Some say it is where the house faces the road – the place of maximum chi; others say it is where the house faces the most unencumbered view, and still others say it is where the main door faces. This matter requires judgement and on-site investigation.

■ Not all experts agree on the prescribed cures for Flying Star afflictions (see pages 93–95). A small minority stubbornly maintains that there are simply no cures other than to move out of afflicted places. Many others use the powerful practice of

symbolic feng shui and five-element theory to prescribe cures for Flying Star afflictions with great success.

So how do you go about determining your own Flying Star chart? The charts used throughout this book as examples in the analyses of home interiors are Period Seven charts. However, Period Seven ends on 4 February 2004, so Period Seven and Period Eight charts are given on pages 88–89. To identify the chart that applies to your house or apartment building, use a compass, stand directly in front of your house and read its facing direction. This tells you which of the 16 charts applies to your house.

CYCLES OF TIME

If you are practising the basic Pa Kua Eight Aspirations method of feng shui (see pages 42–55), the age of your home is irrelevant. However, the more powerful formulas take account of the age of buildings and the changing energy over periods of time.

A full era of time takes 180 years, and this comprises three cycles lasting 60 years each – the Lower, Middle and Upper cycle. Each of these cycles is further divided into 20-year periods, and each period is ruled by a dominant number known as the reigning number. In any period there are 16 different natal charts.

The 20-year Period Seven began on 4 February 1984, and all houses and buildings built, completed or renovated within this period are referred to as Period Seven houses, and the Period Seven natal charts on page 88 represent maps of luck sectors of such houses.

Even if your house or apartment was built at any time before 1984, any renovation or repainting carried out during Period Seven could have transformed it into a Period Seven building. Also, although Period Seven comes to an end on 4 February 2004, for purposes of analysis the natal chart of your home continues to be the Period Seven chart unless you carry out major renovations to turn it into a Period Eight house. However, the meanings of some of the numbers change when the period changes, so it is necessary to start thinking about the forthcoming change to Period Eight, which will run until 4 February 2024.

Period **7**	Period **8**	Period **9**
1984 2004	2004 2024	2024 2044

LEFT Each period lasts 20 years. Period Seven ends on 4 February 2004, when Period Eight begins. It will last for 20 years.

THE 24 MOUNTAINS OF DIRECTIONS

The 24 Mountains is the name given to describe the 24 compass directions in Flying Star feng shui – each of the eight main directions is subdivided into three sub-directions. Thus south is south 1, south 2 and south 3, west is west 1, west 2 and west 3 and so on. Each sub-direction occupies 15 degrees of the compass. To help you determine your facing direction and find the chart that applies to your house, refer to the table below. If yours is a Period Seven building, the Flying Star chart that maps out the luck of your house can be found in this chapter, and you can use your house chart to analyze the feng shui of your home, then design your interiors to benefit from maximum wealth and relationship luck.

FACING DIRECTION OF BUILDING OR FACING DIRECTION OF MAIN DOOR*	THE EXACT READING IN DEGREES READ FROM A RELIABLE COMPASS	FACING DIRECTION OF BUILDING OR FACING DIRECTION OF MAIN DOOR*	THE EXACT READING IN DEGREES READ FROM A RELIABLE COMPASS
South 1	157.5 to 172.5	North 1	337.5 to 352.5
South 2	172.5 to 187.5	North 2	352.5 to 007.5
South 3	187.5 to 202.5	North 3	007.5 to 022.5
Southwest 1	202.5 to 217.5	Northeast 1	022.5 to 037.5
Southwest 2	217.5 to 232.5	Northeast 2	037.5 to 052.5
Southwest 3	232.5 to 247.5	Northeast 3	052.5 to 067.5
West 1	247.5 to 262.5	East 1	067.5 to 082.5
West 2	262.5 to 277.5	East 2	082.5 to 097.5
West 3	277.5 to 292.5	East 3	097.5 to 112.5
Northwest 1	292.5 to 307.5	Southeast 1	112.5 to 127.5
Northwest 2	307.5 to 322.5	Southeast 2	127.5 to 142.5
Northwest 3	322.5 to 337.5	Southeast 3	142.5 to 157.5

* Those living in apartments should determine the facing direction of the whole building and then use the relevant natal chart to analyze the individual apartment. Always use the compass to identify the directions and sectors. You can also identify where your apartment is located in the building's Lo Shu chart. This gives you the general idea of the luck of your apartment, since you can see instantly if the numbers in that grid are auspicious or not. This is one sure way of identifying the lucky apartments in any building.

GETTING THE MOST FROM THE CHARTS

What you want to get from these charts is how to use Flying Star to improve your own feng shui. So what you really want to know is:

■ which stars stand for wealth and which ones stand for relationship luck?

■ which are the lucky and unlucky numbers and how can they be enhanced or remedied?

First, you will need to familiarize yourself with a typical chart. Below is a explanation of what the different numbers in the charts mean and how to read them.

1 The combinations of all the numbers inside each grid are important. The little numbers on the left and right of the big central number are the mountain stars (on the left) and the water stars (on the right). These numbers indicate relationship and wealth luck respectively, and are the important star numbers.

2 The interpretation of charts also takes account of how period number impact on the numbers of the water star and mountain star. The period star is the big number in the centre.

3 Good water star numbers are activated by the presence of yang water. If wealth is what you want, look for where the water star 8 is and then build or buy a beautiful water feature to place there. Invest in one of those really beautiful water features that allow you to have fish, moving water and plants.

4 Good mountain star numbers are activated with earth element objects. If romance is what you want or you wish to strengthen your marriage, or you or your partner are in politics and you want to ensure continued support, then look for the mountain star 8 in your home and in that corner or room place a large natural crystal. Or invest in a large porcelain figurine or stone sculpture, or hang a painting or picture of a mountain range. This will not only vastly improve your relationship luck but also your health. The best energizers are large natural crystals in their original state or large round crystal balls.

5 Do not forget to assess the impact of the month and year star numbers. These exert their influence on the sectors, and when there is a concentration of bad numbers on a particular month, any negative effect is much empowered. Use the feng shui horoscope (see pages 36–37) to factor in the effects of the month and year numbers on the map luck of your house.

6 Finally, note that when bad stars or good stars combine, they usually require a catalyst – an external feature or structure – to trigger an effect. Thus external forms and structures combine with Flying Star to speed up good and bad effects. Symbolic decorative pieces have a vital triggering effect on your luck. When a bad annual star flies into a sector with unlucky natal chart numbers, bad luck gets triggered much faster if a poison arrow (see page 148) is also hurting the sector.

PERIOD SEVEN CHARTS

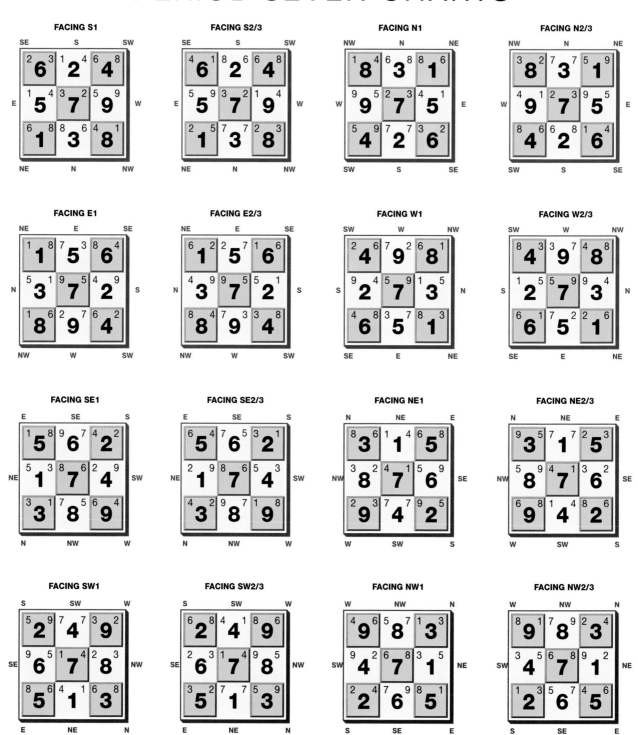

PERIOD EIGHT CHARTS

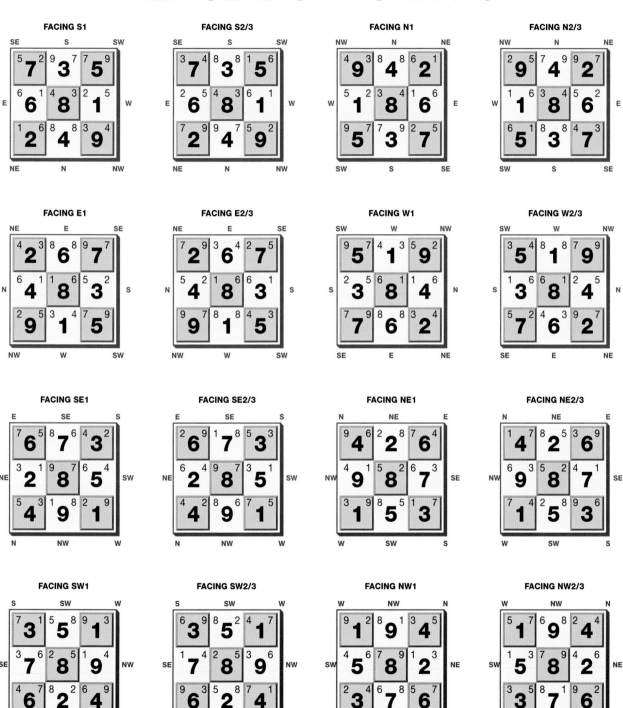

INTERPRETING FLYING STAR CHARTS

Once you know the correct Flying Star chart for your house, focus in on the numbers that occupy your bedroom as well as the 'Facing Palace', which is the hall area near the main door. When the numbers here are auspicious the whole house benefits you and your family.

To start using Flying Star charts, follow this step-by-step approach.

■ Identify the chart that applies to your house.

■ Superimpose all the numbers onto your floor plan correctly.

■ Refer to the tables on pages 96–99 to understand the meanings of the numbers.

■ Place suitable cures wherever necessary to overcome the bad star numbers.

Flying Star feng shui charts are easy to understand once you know the meanings of the lucky and unlucky numbers. Furthermore, by studying the numbers of the water and mountain stars in the particular chart that applies to your house or apartment, you will be able to practise awesomely potent feng shui. For instance, you can determine which rooms have wealth luck and which have loss luck. You can then energize or suppress accordingly using the recommended cures and energizers. Flying Star charts reveal good and bad sectors.

The auspicious numbers in any Flying Star chart are the white numbers 1, 6 and 8, with 8 being the most auspicious. In this current period of 7, the number 7 is also a lucky number but when the period changes on 4 February 2004, the number 8 becomes fantastically auspicious, while the luck of the number 7 will change and will bring burglaries, accidents and loss instead of prosperity. This is why many feng shui enthusiasts who know about Flying Star feng shui are investigating their options on what to do to get ready for Period Eight. In simple Flying Star feng shui, what you need is to take note of the good and bad numbers in the charts.

Mountain and water stars
You must differentiate between the mountain star and the water star. The water star is the facing star and the mountain star is the sitting star. These two stars are the vital luck indicators of the Flying Star chart. Their numbers are very indicative of the luck of the sectors they occupy.

Mountain star
The mountain star is usually placed on the left side of the period number. This

little number here indicates relationship and health luck. If the number is 8, it suggests excellent relationship luck, which will be activated if there is a mountain nearby. Inside the house you can place a large natural crystal in the appropriate area. A feature wall or special boulder is also effective.

Water star

The water star is placed on the right side of the period number. This little number in each of the nine squares of the chart will indicate if the space in that area has wealth chi. If the number is 8 it indicates maximum wealth luck. If it is 5 or 2, it indicates bad luck with money. So looking for the 8 water star is the key to wealth. When you find your water star 8, activate it with a gurgling water feature – it is as simple as that!

ABOVE A water feature placed in the corner where the water star 8 is located in your home or garden will bring you awesome luck.

NUMBER MEANINGS	
5 and 2	The danger numbers to fear are 5 and 2 because these two numbers are described as the sickness numbers. Wherever they appear in any chart, residents who stay or sleep in those sectors will suffer ill luck, get sick or suffer misfortune.
3	The number 3 is a hostile number and it brings misunderstandings, quarrels and fighting. If the 3 hits your room you could be slammed with a lawsuit.
4	The number 4 is lucky for romance and brings literary luck in Period Seven but will turn unlucky in Period Eight. It must not be too near water as this can lead to sex scandals.
9	The number 9 is a magnifying number and has the power to magnify the ill effects of 5 and 2. It is to be feared when it occurs with these two numbers. But on its own it is a very good number, encompassing the completeness of heaven and earth.
7	The number 7 is lucky in this period but turns dangerous and bloody in the next period, bringing burglary, robbery and fatal accidents.
1, 6 and 8	The numbers 1, 6 and 8 are the most auspicious numbers, but it is the number 8 that is truly, awesomely auspicious. The energy of 6 is weak and needs to be activated.

MAPPING THE LUCK OF AN APARTMENT

When you use Flying Star formula feng shui to analyze the luck sectors of apartments, the chart to use is the one that coincides with the facing direction of the whole building and not the entrance to the apartment. Once you have determined this chart, you then superimpose it onto the apartment layout plan according to the compass directions. This uses the application of the small tai chi (see page 45).

Shown below is a Period Seven west 1 chart. It has three auspicious rooms – the family room which has the water star 8, the master bedroom which has the mountain star 8 and the living room which has the extremely lucky three number combination of 1, 6 and 8. Residents of this apartment will definitely enjoy good fortune since the key rooms are so auspicious. But the main entrance area has the water star 5 and this is an affliction that must be overcome. It is vital to hang a metallic wind chime in this part of the apartment to dissolve the evil influence of the water star 5 at the entrance. Simply by doing this, residents are guarded against bad luck and can enjoy the good luck brought by the strategic occurrence of lucky water and mountain stars in the bedrooms and living room.

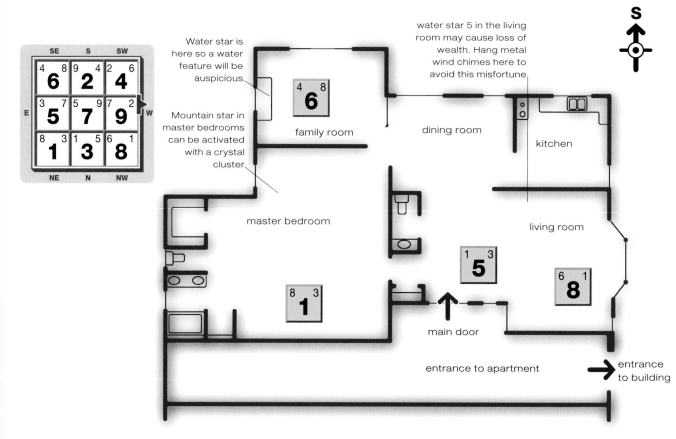

Water star is here so a water feature will be auspicious.

Mountain star in master bedrooms can be activated with a crystal cluster.

water star 5 in the living room may cause loss of wealth. Hang metal wind chimes here to avoid this misfortune.

family room

dining room

kitchen

master bedroom

living room

main door

entrance to apartment

entrance to building

OVERCOMING AFFLICTIONS

Flying Star is an excellent method for preventing bad luck caused by afflictions. Afflictions manifest as illness, loss, failure and the breakup of relationships. These are based on the intangible forces of time and they cause health as well as material, physical and financial problems. Feng shui practice involves identifying these afflictions and protecting against their occurrence. Remedies require clever use of the five-element theory. Thus symbols representing water, fire, wood, earth and metal can be used with great potency to disarm the 5/2s, 5/9s and 3/2s of negative Flying Star number combinations.

The example illustrated here shows a Flying Star chart superimposed onto the layout plan of a two-level townhouse. This is a Period Seven house facing north 2/3. The chart reveals four afflicted sectors in this house (shown in red) and the chart

repeats itself on both levels. In the east, the upstairs master bedroom has the 5/5 water/time star combination that brings loss of wealth and the 9/5 as the mountain/time star numbers, bringing bad luck in relationships. Hanging wind chimes here will control these negative numbers. Downstairs, these numbers are in the garage so here the affliction is not serious. But upstairs, in the master bedroom, metal energy must be used to weaken the 9/5 – otherwise the couple will suffer relationship problems and illness. In the second bedroom, we see the quarrelsome combination of 3/2 signifying the mountain/water stars. This bedroom will cause anyone staying here to become very quarrelsome and to encounter hostility from others. It is better to move to another bedroom, such as the room that has the double 7. Since it is still Period Seven, this is a much luckier bedroom.

BELOW AND LEFT Since Flying Star charts are excellent for highlighting afflicted energy in the different corners of your apartment or house, Flying Star is the best feng shui method for preventing bad luck.

BACK ALLEY

UPSTAIRS

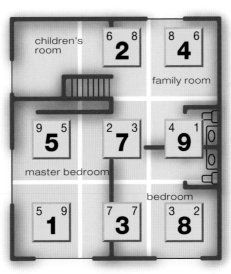

OVERCOMING ILLNESS STARS 2 AND 5

From the charts, you will see that the numbers 2 and 5 are the two illness stars, which can be quite deadly when they come together into any sector of the house. Of these two numbers, 2 brings illness and 5 brings loss, accidents and misfortunes. The deadly 5 is a number to be most feared in

time dimension feng shui. It is important at the start of each HSIA calendar year (see page 37) to check where the annual 5 is. In feng shui terminology, this is referred to as the deadly five yellow (see page 102).

In 2003 the five yellow is in the southeast and in 2004 it flies to the centre. If your front door is located in either of these directions, you can protect against the five yellow in this important part of the house by hanging a six-rod all metal wind chime. The sound of metal on metal is a very powerful cure. The wind chime becomes even more powerful when it has six rods because six is the number of big metal. A five-rod wind chime can be effective, although it is far less powerful than the six-rod variety. Also, hollow rods are usually better than solid ones. This enables the chi to move up through the rods, transforming bad energy into good.

Metal wind chimes are also excellent for controlling the illness star 2, because 2 is an earth element number. The metal wind chime will exhaust the earth energy of the 2. If your bedroom is occupied by the number (the 2 is in the north sector in 2003), you can also place six metal I-Ching coins near your bed, preferably by the side of the bed.

Wind chimes should be hung along the side of the room, but never directly above the bed, since you do not want to be sleeping under a wind chime. Wind chimes should not be hung over a doorway, either, except when the five yellow afflicts the main door. Then it can be hung over the doorway, although feng shui masters in Hong Kong believe that sticking six large coins above the doorway is a better remedy.

RIGHT To overcome the illness star 2 and misfortune star 5, it is best to use an all-metal wind-chime with six rods. Although the wind chime shown here has six rods, the wooden plank above the rods is not as suitable as it would be if it was made of metal.

SUBDUING THE QUARRELLING STAR

In time-dimension feng shui, the number 3 is said to create aggressive energy. This is the quarrelling star that can lead to misunderstandings, hostility and, in extreme cases, court battles. When the number 3 is doubled in any sector (in that it occurs in the trigram chart and also the annual chart), the afflicted sector will see a surplus of this hostile energy. This is usually the cause of marital strife and loud arguments between siblings and members of any household. When the 3 is combined with the 2, the effect of quarrelling becomes worse and can lead to separations.

To subdue the 3 star, it is best to use silent cures that exhaust the element essence of the number without destroying the growth energy of its intrinsic wood element. Thus the colour red used in small quantities can be most effective. Bright lights would be too strong. One of the best cures for the 3/2 are Happiness Buddha images in red and gold.

LEFT Look for a Laughing Happiness Buddha as shown here, wearing red robes and carrying an ingot to subdue the quarrelsome number 3 star.

Candles floating in water are an ideal cure for subduing the number 3's aggressive nature. Place them on tables in sectors afflicted with the number 3 star.

Another excellent cure would be a painting of red goldfish in a metallic paint. This is especially good for countering a 3/2 combination as it uses fire and metal energy to subdue the aggressive nature of this combination.

Do not place moving objects such as fans, stereo systems and wind chimes in sectors of the home that are afflicted by the number 3 star.

LEFT Three candles floating in water is a suitable way to subdue the quarrelsome 3 star but the Laughing Happiness Buddha with red robes is a superior cure.

95

MOUNTAIN AND WATER STAR COMBINATIONS

MOUNTAIN STAR	WATER STAR	INDICATED OUTCOMES OF THE COMBINATION IN PERIODS SEVEN AND EIGHT	ENHANCERS TO TRIGGER GOOD LUCK OR SUPPRESS BAD LUCK COMBINATIONS
1	2	Marriage problems caused by dominating women. A water number as mountain star is a sign of danger similar to a mountain falling into water – a bad sign indeed.	Use plants to exhaust the bad water star and fire energy to strengthen the earth element of the good mountain star. Here the need is to strengthen relationships and guard against losses.
2	1	The matriarch is too strong, leading to marital problems.	Use metal to exhaust the earth. Wind chimes. Place water feature here.
1	3	Wealth and fame luck are indicated but lawsuits and gossip cause aggravation.	Use water plants to enhance and still water to diffuse misunderstandings caused by afflicted water star.
3	1	Prosperity luck is good, but if you don't have the karma/luck to live here you will change residence.	Plant a bamboo grove in front of the house to strengthen your luck. Also place water to activate the water star.
1	4	Political luck. Media and publicity luck. Romance luck for women.	Use slow-moving water but not too much. Plants are also good.
4	1	Romance luck but too much water leads to sex scandals. Affairs leading to unhappiness and breakup of family. Literary success.	Use plants to strengthen the wood element of mountain star and small amount of water to activate the water star for prosperity.
1	5	Health problems dealing with the womb, the kidneys and food poisoning.	Use wind chimes to overcome the 5 and exhaust the 1 mountain star.
5	1	Hearing problems and sex-related illness. Ear diseases.	Use wind chimes to overcome these afflictions.
1	6	Auspicious for second son. There will be scholastic success and intelligence combined with great commercial skills.	Enhance with metal – wind chimes, coins, bells and other auspicious symbols.
6	1	Known as 'peach-blossom luck'. Financial luck and high achievers in the family.	Enhance with metal – wind chimes, coins, bells and other auspicious symbols.
1	7	Good money luck in Period Seven only, in Period Eight this combination means loss of wealth.	Enhance with crystals or gem tree. The best enhancer would be citrines or crystals and lights.
7	1	Extremely good prosperity luck in Period Seven but luck turns bad in Period Eight – danger of burglary.	Use boulders in Period Seven and in Period Eight use a water feature.
1	8	Excellent wealth and prosperity luck in Period Eight. Must activate.	Enhance with water feature to activate water star 8.
8	1	Excellent and auspicious luck. Money and family luck.	Enhance with boulder and crystals to enhance relationship luck.
1	9	Good combination but can turn bad when the annual star 5 flies in.	Do not enhance. When 5 flies in use wind chimes.
9	1	Some good luck but danger of heart problems and sex diseases. Constant changing of jobs.	Do not disturb, but when 5 flies in as annual star use wind chimes.

THE FLYING STAR FORMULA

MOUNTAIN STAR	WATER STAR	INDICATED OUTCOMES OF THE COMBINATION IN PERIODS SEVEN AND EIGHT	ENHANCERS TO TRIGGER GOOD LUCK OR SUPPRESS BAD LUCK COMBINATIONS
2	3	Arguments and misunderstandings of the most severe kind. Back-stabbing, hatred, legal disputes.	Use still water to cool tempers. Do not disturb. Room is best avoided when these numbers appear.
3	2	Dangerous for those in politics. Problems with matriarch. Females afflicted. Best to avoid this room.	Some masters recommend gold and fire. Also still water. Goldfish painted on gold paper is an excellent cure.
2	4	Wives and mothers-in-law quarrel and fight. Disharmony in love.	Use water to overcome mountain star 2 and plants to enhance 4.
4	2	Problems with internal organs. Husband has affairs. Mother-in-law problems.	Use water to reduce stress.
2	5	Extremely dangerous to health. A situation of total loss financially. A catastrophe. A most dangerous combination and when annual 5 flies in, anyone staying here will suddenly have accident or develop terminal illness.	Use wind chimes, moving metallic objects like clocks or fans, and coins. Metal sound is powerful to overcome this combination. Beware: do not have fire or bright spotlights as this can lead to bankruptcy and even death.
5	2	Misfortunes and extreme bad luck. Illness may be fatal. Be very wary.	Use wind chimes, etc, as above. Better to move out of this room.
2	6	Life of ease and leisure. This auspicious combination is spoilt if a five-rod wind chime is placed here.	Do not spoil the luck here with wind chimes. Said to attract earth spirits! Activate the water star with water, which also suppresses the 2 mountain star.
6	2	Great affluence and success.	Place a boulder to strengthen the mountain star.
2	7	There is wealth during Period Seven, but luck of children is bad. Problems conceiving children. In Period Eight there are many problems. When annual star 9 enters, things get worse.	Use metal (bells) in Period Seven and use water in Period Eight. When 9 enters as annual star, place a large urn of water or there could be a fire.
7	2	Money luck dissipates. Children luck is dimmed. In Period Eight mountain 7 brings much bad luck.	Use wind chimes to exhaust and water to suppress the 7 mountain star in Period Eight.
2	8	Richness and wealth, but there is ill health. This can be remedied. Excellent water star.	Use water to overcome bad health star and simultaneously activate the 8 water star.
8	2	Mountain star 8 brings relationship luck. But water star 2 brings loss.	Use mountain principle to strengthen mountain and weaken water.
2	9	Peach-blossom luck for women. Romance does not last. Nothing succeeds unless remedied.	Use water plants to disarm bad mountain star and also balance effect of 9 water star.
9	2	Problems with children but good relationship luck.	Better to do nothing. Use metal to control the 2 water star.

MOUNTAIN STAR	WATER STAR	INDICATED OUTCOMES OF THE COMBINATION IN PERIODS SEVEN AND EIGHT	ENHANCERS TO TRIGGER GOOD LUCK OR SUPPRESS BAD LUCK COMBINATIONS
3	4	Danger of mental instability. Mature women get stressed. Theft.	Use bright lights to exhaust the wood element. Be wary of excesses.
4	3	Emotional stress because of relationship problems. Stress.	Use red to overcome stress, but not naked flames.
3	5	Loss of wealth. Severe cash-flow problems. If bedroom is here, financial loss is severe. If kitchen is here, sickness is inevitable.	Exhaust the 5 with metal but not with wind chimes or bells. Use copper mountain painting. Better not to stay in this part of the house.
5	3	Money troubles. Disputes. Bad business luck. Bad for sons.	Use still (yin) water to disarm the mountain star 5 and control the 3 water star.
3	6	Period of slow growth. Problems with limbs. Danger of accidents.	Use still (yin) water.
6	3	Danger of betrayal by friends. Danger of car accidents.	Balance with real crystal gemstones.
3	7	Robberies or burglaries. Violence. Not too bad in Period Seven but acute in Period Eight.	Use still (yin) water to overcome the effect of this dangerous combination. Place Laughing Buddha here to disarm.
7	3	Grave danger of injury to limbs. Be careful. Also car accidents and theft.	Use still (yin) water. Place Laughing Buddha here to disarm.
3	8	Not good for children under 12 years.	Use bright lights to cure the 3 but activate water star 8 with water.
8	3	Move children under 12 away from this sector or accidents happen.	Activate mountain star 8 with big crystal or wall or boulder.
4	5	Prone to sexually transmitted diseases. Breast cancer. Bad skin.	Control the 5 with wind chimes and other metal. Combination is bad.
5	4	Skin diseases and severe illness.	Use water/mountain and wind chimes.
4	6	Bad luck for women who will bear heavy burdens. Miscarriage.	Strengthen earth element. Use water to activate water star.
6	4	Unexpected windfall for women of the family and excellent romance.	Enhance with wind chime and crystals. Activate with dragon image.
4	7	Bad luck in love. Will get cheated by opposite sex. Miscarriage.	Use yang water as remedy for this combination. Paint walls blue.
7	4	Taken for a ride by someone of the opposite sex. Also cheated.	Use yang water. Install lights to remedy danger of being cheated.
4	8	Bad for very young children but water star 8 here brings prosperity.	Use lights to combat effect on children and activate water star with water.
8	4	Overpowering matriarch. Love life of younger generation will suffer from the wiles of the mother.	Use fire, or red to overcome. Also activate mountain star 8 with boulder or crystal. Activate with dragon image.
4	9	A time for preparation. Good for sons who excel at school. Bad for daughters. Danger of fire.	Use plants. Also goldfish. Activate with crystal globe and dragon image.
9	4	Good luck for those starting new business. Benefits sons.	Use water to enhance. Add goldfish and image of dragon.

MOUNTAIN STAR	WATER STAR	INDICATED OUTCOMES OF THE COMBINATION IN PERIODS SEVEN AND EIGHT	ENHANCERS TO TRIGGER GOOD LUCK OR SUPPRESS BAD LUCK COMBINATIONS
5	7	Problems caused by excessive gossiping. Danger of poisoning or anything to do with the mouth.	Use metal in Period Seven and water in Period Eight.
7	5	Mouth-related problems. Arguments leading to emotional stress.	Use metal in Period Seven and water in Period Eight. Also use plants to combat the 5 water star.
5	8	Problems related to the limbs, joints and bones of the body. Danger of paralysis. It is necessary to be careful of rough sports. Emotional problems. But water star 8 is here.	Use still (yin) water to pacify. The water star here is auspicious and must be activated. So water is the best feature here.
8	5	There is danger of paralysis and illness of a serious nature. But the mountain star 8 here is auspicious.	Strengthen the mountain star 8 with large natural crystal but also hang wind chime here to fight the five yellow.
5	9	Bad luck and tempers. Excessive mental disorder or stress – there is unhappiness and dissatisfaction.	Use wind chime here to combat the strengthening of the five yellow by the 9. Water/mountain theory.
9	5	Very bad indications of health and also for loss of wealth through gambling. Possible problems with eyes. Stubborn people.	Use wind chimes, as this is really the best cure for this combination of numbers. Always beware of the 5/9 and 9/5 combinations.
6	7	'Sword fighting killing breath'. A case of double metal clashing – daughter and father fight. Daughter causes loss of face and honour.	Use still (yin) water to control. Important to disarm the water star with fire energy. Bright lights are a good idea here.
7	6	Jealousy and constant arguments. Father and daughter have serious arguments.	Use still (yin) water to control. Important to disarm the water star with fire energy. Bright lights are a good idea here.
6	8	Wealth, popularity, prosperity. Great richness. Probably the best combination in Flying Star technique. Water star 8 is most auspicious.	Enhance with water and make sure you have an entrance or window in that sector to invite in the prosperity.
8	6	A great combination, which holds the promise of good relationship luck, popularity and recognition.	Enhance the mountains star with a large boulder or sculpture. It will be very auspicious indeed.
6	9	Fire at heaven's gate. Arguments and danger of fire. Must not have kitchen here or there will be fire.	Look for a wide-mouth container and fill with water – to reduce danger of fire causing wealth loss.
9	6	Same as above. Danger to family. Patriarch must not stay here.	Same cure as above to reduce danger of spoilt reputation and loss of popularity.
7	9	Extreme problems during Period Eight. All troubles caused through excessive vulnerability to sexual advances. Danger of fire hazards.	Use water or earth (big boulders) to press down on the bad luck. A very dangerous combination when period changes to Period Eight.
9	7	Problems arise from extreme flirtatious tendency. Fire is a danger.	Use still (yin) water to control both the 7 and 9, especially during Period Eight.
8	9	Joyous and happy. Good indication for marriage to those who stay here.	No need to activate any more, but if you want marriage display a double happiness image.
9	8	Excellent indication of happiness occasion. Excellent for marital bliss.	No need to activate further.

REGULAR UPDATING OF YOUR FENG SHUI

To truly safeguard the luck of your abode and guard against misfortunes, it is a good idea to undertake annual updates to your time dimension feng shui. It is not a difficult exercise once you know exactly what to do and how to move the cures and remedies around the house.

When you are carrying out your annual feng shui update, there are three important annual afflictions of which you should be aware and take action to counter. These are the deadly five yellow, the Grand Duke Jupiter and the three killings.

The compass map shown below indicates the locations of the afflictions in the year 2004 (from 4 February 2004 to 3 February 2005). A new map is needed for each new year, because each year the location of these three afflictions change, and the basis of this change differs for each one of the afflictions.

Feng shui masters in the East focus on these afflictions when carrying out annual updates for their clients, otherwise the afflictions, especially the five yellow, could be serious enough to cause sudden loss and bankruptcy of their business. Sometimes annual afflictions can also cause terminal illness to strike.

Note that each of the three afflictions occupies different angles in terms of degrees – the Grand Duke occupies only 15 degrees, the five yellow occupies 45 degrees and the three killings occupies 90 degrees – so the extent of their impact on the floor area of houses and buildings will differ.

There are antidotes for controlling or overcoming these afflictions, depending on where they are each year. There are also safeguards that can be used according to locations afflicted. To ensure protection from the ill effect of these annual afflictions, the first thing to take note of is their location from year to year. The second thing to note is the taboos – what you simply must not do so as not to incur the wrath of the afflictions. The five yellow brings major financial loss and fatal illnesses, the three killings bring three kinds of bad luck associated with relationships, while the Grand Duke brings defeat and failure. Knowing about these afflictions will help you to evade their ill effects.

RIGHT This chart shows you the location of the three afflictions in 2004. Please note that the deadly five yellow occupies the centre of any building.

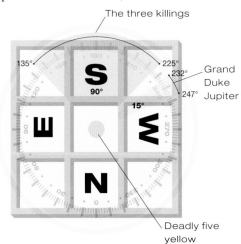

The three killings

135°

225°
232°
247°
Grand Duke Jupiter

15°

S 90°

E

W 270°

N

Deadly five yellow

NEVER OFFEND THE GRAND DUKE JUPITER

The Grand Duke Jupiter (also known as the tai tsui) affects 15 degrees of space that corresponds to the direction of the animal sign of the year. So in 2003 it flies to the southwest, which is the corresponding direction of the Sheep, and all taboos with respect to the Grand Duke apply to the direction southwest.

Firstly, no one should sit directly facing southwest, even though southwest may be very lucky for you under the Kua formula, since this is interpreted as challenging the Grand Duke. When you confront the Grand Duke you will lose, you will be defeated and you will get sick. Instead, you should sit with the Grand Duke behind you. This way, you will get support. So in 2003, by sitting with the southwest behind you and thus facing northeast, you will be strengthened in whatever you do because you will then have the support of the God of the Year, as the Grand Duke is often referred to.

Secondly, you should not disturb the peace and quiet of the Grand Duke's palace. This means that in 2003 you should not play loud music or quarrel in the southwest; nor should you undertake renovations, banging, digging and demolition work here. If you do, the result will be loss, bad luck and illness. This vital taboo applies if you are planning to undertake spot renovations in the home, and each year you must take note of the parts of your home where you should not undertake any renovation work.

In 2004 the Grand Duke will occupy the direction of the Monkey, which is southwest, and in 2005 he will occupy the direction of the Rooster, which is west. The chart illustrates the directions of the Grand Duke indicated for the next 12 years. Once you know where to find the Grand Duke each year, it is easy enough to observe the taboos associated with him.

Note also that those born in the animal year directly opposite to the ruling animal are said to be in direct conflict with the Grand Duke. So in 2003, Ox year people are in conflict, as the Ox is opposite the Sheep. To cure this affliction, place an image of the Pi Yao, a celestial animal that offers protection, in the Grand Duke's location.

BELOW This chart shows you how to find the location of the Grand Duke each year. Its location is the 15 degrees of space that correspond to the animal sign of the year.

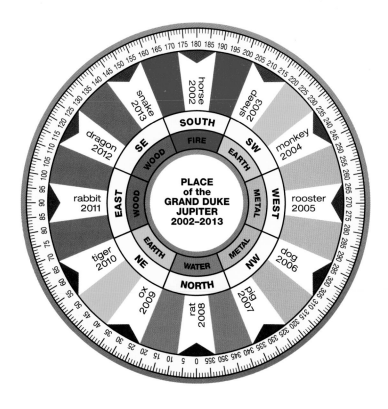

BEWARE THE DEADLY FIVE YELLOW

The five yellow is the most deadly of the three annual afflictions, especially in years when it flies into earth and fire element sectors, such as in 1999 when it flew to the south, a fire element sector, and in 2001 when it flew into the southwest, an earth element sector. In these two sectors the evil essence of the five yellow, being an earth element affliction, was considerably strengthened, bringing severe illness, financial loss and obstacles to success.

The five yellow is at its deadliest when it afflicts the main door or your bedroom. In 2001, when the five yellow flew into the southwest, both my main door and my bedroom were afflicted. In December of that year I discovered I had a number of health problems. When I checked my feng shui I realized I had hung six wind chimes at my door, but had forgotten my bedroom was also in the southwest. I lost no time in quickly placing wind chimes there. In February 2002 my doctor was amazed when blood tests indicated that I had recovered. This experience really strengthened my confidence in the Flying Star feng shui system.

Do not take the ill effects of the five yellow lightly – it can be deadly when it hits you. Try never to occupy rooms afflicted by the five yellow, but if you cannot help it, then make sure you use remedies to overcome its effects. You must also not undertake renovations in your home if the five yellow is at your front door, and certainly you must not dig or demolish any part of the home afflicted by it.

The best way to counter the ill effects of the five yellow is to hang six-rod, all-metal hollow wind chimes, as the sound made by metal on metal exhausts the earth chi of the five yellow. Feng shui masters always recommend using the exhausting cycle of the five elements rather than the destructive cycle to control the five yellow affliction. Wind chimes are an excellent antidote because they engage the power of the winds, but you can also place six metal coins above the doorway, or six coins on either side of the door to exhaust the power of the five yellow. However, in 2003 the five yellow is in the southeast, the place of the wood element. Using the traditional cure of the metal wind chime here can destroy the intrinsic wood element of the southeast sector, so use a wind chime only if you feel the affliction strongly, such as when your main door is affected; otherwise let the wood chi control the five yellow on its own, and keep the corner undisturbed throughout the year.

Wherever the five yellow occurs in any home or building, it is important to keep the lights there dimmed. This is because the fire chi will strengthen its earth energy, making it even more deadly.

ABOVE Metal coins are excellent to counter the horrible effects of the five yellow. To activate, just place in the afflicted sector.

PLACE OF THE DEADLY FIVE YELLOW 2002-2012	
2003	SOUTHEAST
2004	CENTRE
2005	NORTHWEST
2006	WEST
2007	NORTHEAST
2008	SOUTH
2009	NORTH
2010	SOUTHWEST
2011	EAST
2012	SOUTHEAST

OVERCOME THE THREE KILLINGS

The last of the annual afflictions is the three killings, known as the sarm saat in Chinese, which brings three kinds of bad luck to relationships. Unlike the Grand Duke Jupiter, who must never be confronted, the three killings must always be faced up to, head on. This means if it occupies the north then you must face the north – to have the three killings behind you is asking to be stabbed in the back. Always rearrange your furniture each new year so that you do not inadvertently have the three killings behind you.

When planning house repairs and renovations, make very sure that you do not undertake such works in sectors of the house occupied by the three killings. This is a troublesome taboo to observe since the three killings can occupy a very large part of the house – this affliction covers 90 degrees of the compass. This is because the three killings only flies to the cardinal directions and never into the secondary directions.

In the years of the Ox, Rooster and Snake, the three killings occupies the east. The cure here is to shine a bright light in the room, or hang a metal wind chime.

In the years of the Pig, Rabbit and Sheep it occupies the west. The cure here is to place open water in this corner, or shine a bright light.

In the years of the Monkey, Rat and Dragon it occupies the south. The cure here is to use crystals or place open water in this corner.

In the years of the Dog, Horse and Tiger it occupies the north. The cure here is to place a strong plant or use the strong earth energy of crystal.

The way to overcome the three killings thus depends on which compass direction it occupies. Cures are always based on the exhausting cycle of the five elements. If you look at the suggested cures for each of the four cardinal locations where the three killings reside, you will see that the symbols used to overcome the killing chi of this annual affliction will exhaust the afflicted element energy of the direction. This is one of the reasons why I place such stress on knowing the theory of the five elements. You do not need to use the cures I suggest, once you understand the basis of my recommendation you can use symbols that are more pleasing to you.

LEFT A green plant would exhaust the water energy of the north sector and thus keep the three killings under control when it occupies the north.

PERIOD SEVEN HOUSE EXAMPLES

Use the examples given in the following pages to learn how to analyze the numbers of the flying star charts. This will enable you to identify the auspicious rooms and the afflicted rooms.

HOUSE FACING SOUTH

A building that faces south 1 enjoys the double 7 in the front of the building, and if the main door were also placed here in this sector it would be very auspicious. The time number is 2 and it is not strong enough to override the auspicious double 7. The water star 8 is in the northeast, so placing a pool or a water feature in the northeast of the living room will activate the lucky water star. The mountain star 8 is in the north at the back of the house, so if there is higher ground behind it would be most auspicious.

For a south 2/3-facing building, the water and mountain star numbers in the grid flip so that the double 7 sector is now in the

north grid at the back of the house. So the master bedroom here has excellent luck. The water star 8 has flipped to the front in the southwest sector, so placing a water feature here brings prosperity. The mountain star 8 has flipped to the front also and is now at the south grid, so placing boulders and stones near the front would be auspicious. East and northeast rooms have the 5/9 and 9/5 combinations, which bring bad luck and need to be controlled with wind chimes. Disarm the 3/2 in the centre with yin water.

BELOW South 1 or south 2/3 facing buildings have some excellent sectors, enjoying the auspicious double 7 as well as the 6/8 and the 8/6. By varying the facing direction by 15 degrees you can change your house from an south 1 to an south 2/3 and vice versa. This has the effect of flipping the lucky double 7 from the front to the back.

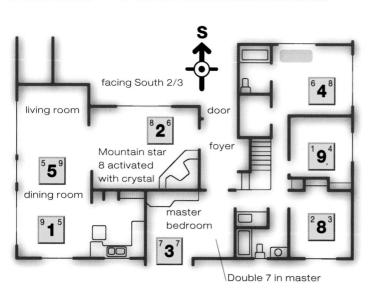

facing South 2/3

living room

door

$^8 2 ^6$

foyer

Mountain star 8 activated with crystal

$^5 5 ^9$

dining room

$^9 1 ^5$

$^6 4 ^8$

$^1 9 ^4$

$^2 8 ^3$

$^7 3 ^7$

master bedroom

Double 7 in master bedroom brings excellent luck in Period 7

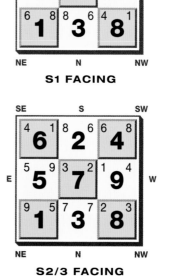

S1 FACING

SE	S	SW
$^2 6 ^3$	$^7 2 ^7$	$^9 4 ^5$
$^1 5 ^4$	$^3 7 ^2$	$^5 9 ^9$
$^6 1 ^8$	$^8 3 ^6$	$^4 8 ^1$

E — W

NE · N · NW

S2/3 FACING

SE	S	SW
$^4 6 ^1$	$^8 2 ^6$	$^6 4 ^8$
$^5 5 ^9$	$^3 7 ^2$	$^1 9 ^4$
$^9 1 ^5$	$^7 3 ^7$	$^2 8 ^3$

E — W

NE · N · NW

SEMI-DETACHED HOUSE FACING NORTH

Here is an example of a semi-detached house facing north that was built in 1999, which makes it a Period Seven house. If you live in a semi-detached house that was built between 1984 and 2004, and your house faces north, then one of the charts here will be the Flying Star chart for your house – take the compass direction and use the table on page 86 to establish whether the north 1 or north 2/3 chart is appropriate. For this example, we shall assume that the house is facing the north 1 direction. To make the analysis easier, I have 'turned the chart' such that north is facing the same direction as the floor plan illustrated.

Next you look at the numbers in the grids and superimpose them onto the

floor plan. This will tell you which part of the house is lucky and which is unlucky. Refer to the table to get the meanings of the numbers of the water stars and mountain stars.

In this example, the entrance door is very lucky because it has the mountain star 8. Placing a crystal here would activate the lucky mountain star. Next you can see that the water star 8 is also in the living room, so a water feature here would bring prosperity into the family. Unfortunately, the 2/3 combination, which causes quarrels, is where the dining table is, so here a Laughing Buddha painted in red and gold will be required as a remedy.

BELOW These Flying Star charts apply to homes that have a north facing direction. The analysis uses the chart facing north 1.

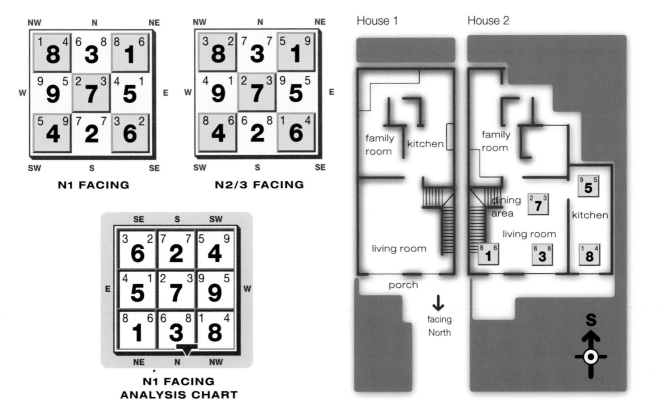

AN L-SHAPED HOUSE FACING NORTHEAST

Here is an L-shaped house that faces northeast 1. However, because it is L-shaped there is a missing corner that occupies two sections. In a situation like this, the numbers that fall outside the house do not affect the interiors, so here, although we actually have two good sets of numbers, the mountain star 8 is outside the house and these good auspicious numbers are thus wasted. However, there are still some good numbers inside the home, for example the double 7 in the dining area near the kitchen

is excellent, although it is not used to its maximum potential in this house. Also, the double 7 turns dangerous in Period Eight.

The 9/5 in the living room must be dealt with. Place a metal wind chime here to control this combination. In the garage, the quarrelsome 2/3 does not do much harm. The water star 8 inside the bedroom is very auspicious but it cannot be activated with water because water in the bedroom causes loss. But the mere presence of the water star 8 makes this an auspicious room.

RIGHT Look closely at how the mountain star 8 is outside the house, so erecting a small concrete wall here would be most beneficial. If this is not installed, the auspicious mountain star is wasted. Note also that the water star 8 is in the master bedroom. Do not activate with water since water in the bedroom is a major taboo in feng shui.

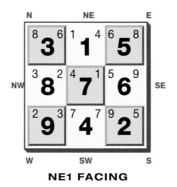

NE1 FACING

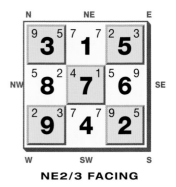

NE2/3 FACING

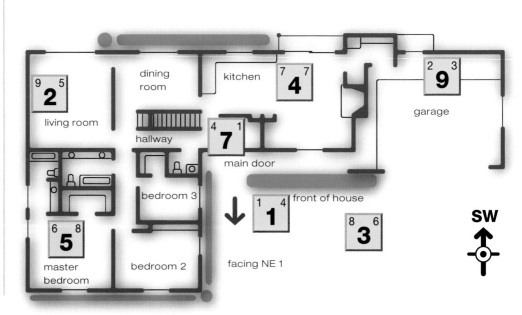

A SOUTHWEST-FACING HOUSE

Period Seven buildings that currently face any one of the three southwest directions, southwest 1, 2 or 3, will have benefited enormously from the double 7, as well as the 6/8 and 8/6 combinations, that feature in these southwest-facing charts.

Those engaged in literary pursuits have benefited from the 4/1 combination, which in a southwest 1 house is in the northeast grid, and in a southwest 2 or 3 house is at the front in the southwest sector itself. This is shown in the example (right). Note also how the pond takes advantage of the water star 8 here. The mountain star 8 shown in the east will be energized with a picture of a mountain. Meanwhile, the quarrelsome combination 3/2 is cured with yin water and the 5/9 is remedied with wind chimes.

Note that houses facing southwest 2 or southwest 3 have the numbers flipped around from houses with a southwest 1 facing direction. The number combinations are the same but they are placed in different grids as shown here.

Southwest houses in Period Eight
I have studied the Period Eight charts and there are some truly auspicious aspects that are said to bring great good fortune during the 20 years from 2004 to 2024. These are mainly houses that face or sit on the southwest/northeast axis. For occupants who know how to activate their good chi, the good luck will be multiplied, especially if there is water in front of the house. So if your house faces either of these directions, it is beneficial to change your home to Period Eight. It is also important for homes facing or sitting in these directions to change to Period Eight because, along with

south- and north-facing homes, they have been benefiting for the last 20 years from the lucky number 7, which in Period Eight reverts to being unlucky.

The change from Period Seven to Eight in February 2004 will have a big effect, not just on houses built or renovated in Period Seven, but on all houses. This is because whenever there is a change in period the energy levels of buildings are instantly affected and Period Seven houses will lose their chi.

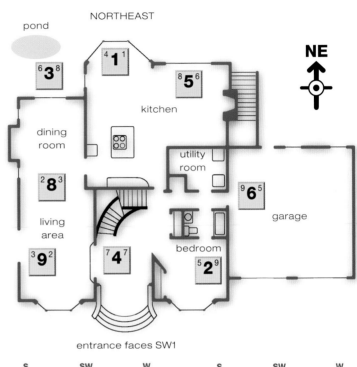

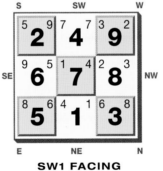

entrance faces SW1

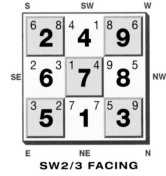

ABOVE Note the water star 8 is in the north. Placing water here is enormously beneficial.

HARMFUL AFFLICTION CURES

Flying Star feng shui is the placement of cures to ward off misfortunes identified by the afflicting numbers, but you must check whether these cures need to be updated annually.

Some combinations of numbers (of the trigram number of the sector and the annual or monthly number) can be very harmful. Residents hit by these combinations will feel the negative effect in the particular month and year when the combination appears. Below are some particularly bad number combinations and what you can do to remedy their ill effects.

Using the grid method (see page 46) to demarcate the sectors of the home, place the suggested cures within the sectors affected by these numbers. Usually, if these negative energy numbers are near the entrance door or in the bedroom, family room or dining room, their ill effects will be felt more strongly. If they are in toilets and storerooms they are in effect 'imprisoned', so cannot cause so much harm. However, if they are in the kitchen, the 5/2, 5/9 and 2/9 will be magnified by the fire energy there. By simply placing an urn of still water in the kitchen, you be able to overcome the ill effects.

CURING NEGATIVE CHI			
2/5 and 5/2	Use metal wind chimes to overcome this very deadly combination. You might need to hang at least six wind chimes or use six large coins. Do not have fire energy here (that is, bright spotlights or the colour red or an open fire).	**2/7 and 7/2**	These combinations are not bad in Period Seven, but are deadly in Period Eight. They are especially harmful to children. An excellent cure is a white porcelain rooster. A sword of coins is also said to be a powerful remedy.
5/5 and 2/2	These are two very critical combinations and extreme danger is always indicated by the double 5, while fatal illness is indicated by the double 2. Again, using six-rod wind chimes would be a powerful cure. Painting the afflicted room white is another excellent way to exhaust the harmful star numbers. You can also use metallic bells and seven-metal singing bowls.	**5/9 and 9/5**	These combinations are to be feared because the 9 magnifies the deadly effects of the 5, so there will be bad luck all round with danger posed to the eyes and limbs. The best remedy against this combination is using metal wind chimes to silence the 5. A gold and red painting can also be effective.
5/3 and 3/5	These combinations cause loss in one's finances leading to severe cash-flow problems. It is important to exhaust the 5 with metal energy, but the metal must be silent so wind chimes are unsuitable. Instead, use a painting of a copper mountain. Yin metal here is an excellent remedy.	**2/3 and 3/2**	These are the quarrelsome combinations. They cause back-stabbing and legal disputes to flare up – a very annoying indication. Use still water to cool the tempers. A silent red flame is also excellent.
3/9 and 9/3	Legal disputes take a turn for the worse. The best cure for this is still water.	**2/4 and 4/2**	These combinations indicate problems involving the in-laws. Use water in an urn to reduce their ill effects.

ENHANCING WITH SYMBOLS

Flying Star feng shui is also about identifying the rooms that have auspicious numbers and enhancing their chi by activating them. The best way to do this is to use symbolic images.

In the same way that negative stars can be remedied and their ill effects somewhat diffused, feng shui also recommends the use of symbolic enhancers that can activate the positive effects of the good star numbers that you may have in certain areas and rooms of your home.

When I first learnt Flying Star and time dimension feng shui, I was thrilled by how easy its practice is, although it was said to be very difficult. In the old days, the classical method of explaining Flying Star feng shui was almost purposely made complicated by the use of special terms in Chinese to refer to the number combinations, as well as the directions and the years. All the different directions and years had special names, and unless one learnt these by heart, it was really confusing to follow the explanations given in the texts. But once I broke the secret code of names it became really easy. This is because the principles of feng shui are so logical and so scientific.

Using symbols to enhance good luck is an amazingly powerful technique. Perhaps it has to do with the energy vibrations that surround these symbols. Maybe when placed strategically according to the distribution of luck in the different sectors of the home they become more effective. Try placing the symbols in different corners of your rooms to activate the good numbers and see if your luck improves.

ABOVE Bedrooms that enjoy the presence of water star 8 should not use water features. A blue bedcover instead would be excellent.

BRINGING OUT THE LUCK

1/1 Use water features to enhance corners of rooms with this number combination. Water-turning crystal balls come in many different designs and are very auspicious. Never put water in bedrooms, however.

6/6 Use metal enhancers such as a gold-plated sailing ship, a silver vase or anything else made of metal. The number 6 is powerful and does not really require enhancing, but a whole harbour of gold ships brings many sources of income!

8/8 The number 8 is a super auspicious number that does not need enhancing, but placing eight crystal balls when the 8 appears brings really great good fortune, harmony and peace. Alternatively, place eight crystal obelisks to attract power.

FENG SHUI IN ACTION

Now you have learnt about all the different feng shui formulas, and how to use the House Trigram and Flying Star charts, you can put it all into practice to help you plan your life and enhance your luck. This chapter is full of ideas to guide you, but by just using the yin and yang principles to ensure there is sufficient yang energy in your home, and applying the five-element principles to ensure there is balance, you will generate many good ideas of your own.

Practising feng shui is never a static activity. Instead, it is a wonderfully dynamic practice that involves keeping the flow of chi moving. You can use the five-element principles to choose colours, shapes and the art you hang on your walls. You can use these principles to choose between metal, wood or stone materials. You can select auspicious decorative objects that symbolize different types of luck, and you can use the secrets of Flying Star feng shui to tap into very potent and intangible forces of chi.

While you cannot do much to change the way mountains, buildings and the external environment align with your home, bringing feng shui into the design of your interiors is feng shui that is definitely within your control. This is practical feng shui – the really good stuff!

THE MAIN DOOR

One of the more powerful feng shui features to have in any house is a personalized main door, whose location and facing direction is personally auspicious for the breadwinner of the house. It may be the man of the house or you can choose to reflect the matriarch's good directions.

RIGHT After selecting the orientation of the main door, the next thing is to use colour to enhance it. Use red for doors located in the southwest, northeast and south. Use black for doors facing east, southeast and north. Use white for doors facing northwest, west and north.

The decision on whose Kua number shall determine the main door direction and location is up to you, but your decision will affect everyone in the house. The reason is that once the main door is positioned in a house design, this usually also defines the facing direction of the whole house. This in turn defines the distribution of chi throughout the house.

There are always choices to be made in feng shui regarding which direction to use as the facing direction, and then which chart to follow. There are always trade-offs involved when deciding on how best to use each of the formulas. This can boil down to simply having to decide which door to use and which room to allocate to which member of the family.

Personalize your main door

The ideal situation is to personalize the main door. By choosing its facing direction you affect the facing direction of the house, and from there you can design the rest of the house based on the natal chart created. This is the essence of good feng shui practice for interior spaces.

Face your good luck directions

If you cannot personalize your door, however, use a door into the house that faces one of your four good directions. This will bring you good luck as you enter your house. It does not have to be the main door. You should try not to use a door that faces one of your four bad directions (if you can help it), since this will cause you to bring bad luck and loss as you enter the house. Even if this means having to use a side door, or the back door, you should observe this advice. If

you live in an apartment block, look for a way to get into the building using a door that brings you good fortune.

Main door should have a roof

The main door should be protected, even if only symbolically. This suggests a small roof above the main door. If you look at the architecture of old homes and inside the palaces of the Forbidden City, you will find that all main entrances have this protective feature. A popular adaptation for modern homes is illustrated here. If your door does not have a protective roof, consider having a canopy made.

Main door should be solid wood

Ideally, main doors should be made of solid wood with some metallic trimmings. The stronger the door, the better it is in terms of protecting the home. Glass doors afford little protection. Gold or brass decorations on doors are excellent. These can fine-tune the compass direction chi of the door itself – you will find the presence of metal studs or lion door knockers can change the direction of any compass reading near the door by a few degrees. This used to be a secret and efficient way to adjust chi direction near the door.

Main door should open inwards

When the main door opens inwards, chi is welcomed into the home. This creates a positive flow of chi at the mouth of the home. It is easy to adjust this if your doors open outward. It is not a good idea to have sliding doors as the main entrance. If you place a mat at the entrance, make sure it is outside and not inside the house, and never put your name on the mat – you don't want to get stepped on, do you?

ABOVE Using a lion-faced door knocker creates excellent protective chi for your main door.

113

A GOOD FLOW OF CHI

The first principle to bear in mind when designing your home interiors is to keep an eye on the way the invisible energy moves inside the home.

This is the famous flow of chi concept that generally determines whether your home feels balanced and harmonious or not. It is how you subconsciously direct the way human traffic moves within the home. It has to do with the way furniture is placed inside rooms so they do not block the flow of chi, and how natural passageways are created that direct people from one part of the home to another, and from room to room.

The flow of chi in any home is auspicious when it flows slowly and in a meandering fashion. Whenever chi flows in a straight line, the area or corridor must always be large enough for the chi to slow down. Hanging a painting or mirror on the side walls will enhance the flow of chi. The flow of chi can also be made to slow down with clever placement of furniture. When spaces are narrow and cramped, do not make matters worse by

TIPS FOR ENHANCING YOUR HOME'S CHI

- Go for a meandering flow rather than a straight line flow.

- Don't have doors in a straight line as this causes a poisonous straight flow.

- Try to make your conduits of chi spacious rather than cramped.

- Let the chi from the outdoors flow freely in. Open your windows.

- Block off unsightly views from your flow of chi – throw out dying plants.

- Don't let energy stagnate at corners, in storerooms or in closets or these areas will succumb to yin spirit formation. Shine a bright light there to counter with yang energy.

- Try to let the energy move diagonally across rooms.

- Let external breezes and sunlight bathe the home in fresh chi.

- Let all the spaces inside the home get activated occasionally. If you have rooms that are not used – for example, bedrooms of children away studying – open the windows regularly, turn on the fan, switch on the stereo or turn on the lights for a while. This will balance the chi and prevent the energy in that room from getting excessively yin.

- Identify parts of the garden that may be ignored and activate the chi there too.

ABOVE This room
has a feeling of space
which is always good
in feng shui. Note the
large mirror on the
right enhances the
space even more.

placing cupboards that cause potential blockage to the flow of chi.

Traffic within any interior space will flow according to the flow of chi, and thus we should try to ensure that it moves naturally from room to room. Generally, the more people there are in any sector or corner of the home, the more yang the energy deposited there will be. Thus high-traffic areas tend to see a higher accumulation of yang energy – and the good sheng chi – than low-traffic areas.

When chi gets blocked, your path in life also gets blocked. As a result, success also gets blocked. It is not so much what furniture or artefacts you put into your rooms, but how you place them, that affects the flow of chi.

Try to map out a route that reflects how people move within the home. By doing this you can identify feng shui afflictions. See where the eye leads you. At the entrance, the flow of traffic should lead to a bright hall and never to staircases and toilets. Look out for rooms that do not get used frequently, and also take note of corners that are ignored and rooms that are hard to get to. The idea is to balance the flow of chi.

AUSPICIOUS ROOM LAYOUT

There are different feng shui methods you can follow when designing the room layout in your home, helping you to decide where to place the rooms, how big to make them and so on. Here is where knowing all your options can make such a difference to eventually having an auspicious house. Below are some of your options.

■ You can use the Eight Mansions formula method to personalize sleeping and sitting directions for different members of the family (see pages 64–65).

■ You may want to select the most auspicious part of the house according to Flying Star feng shui so you can be sure that your master bedroom is located in the part of the house with the best star numbers (see pages 82–109).

■ You may wish to arrange house layout according to the Pa Kua method, focusing on the kind of luck you want for your bedroom (see pages 42–55).

■ You may even want to select the rooms according to the Pa Kua's allocation of spaces to different members of the family, for example, the father in the northwest, sons in the east and so on.

All the different methods of feng shui work, and some work very well. The advantage in personally knowing the different methods is that it is you who will decide between several options rather than an indifferent consultant. Also, by knowing feng shui, you will have the confidence to discuss more intelligently with your architect and interior designer what you want.

Knowing Flying Star feng shui enables you to change the energy of the home based on its orientation. So you see how flexible feng shui can be when practised in a smart way. There is really a great deal of common sense in feng shui. I really believe that many of the different methods of feng shui are valid and have something to offer – even those that have been adapted for modern living. There is no need to be dogmatic about ancient feng shui knowledge. Many Western New Age practitioners demonstrate genuinely wonderful insights that even seasoned masters with many years of experience have failed to pick up.

RIGHT Learning about auspicious room layout will enable you to look at the interior design of your home with fresh eyes.

SELECTING AUSPICIOUS FURNITURE

Selecting auspicious furniture plays an important role in improving your feng shui. Your furniture should always give you support, and it is important for the family patriarch to sit in chairs with armrests to ensure that he is never lacking in support.

Furniture should never block the flow of chi, so there should not be so much furniture as to create a feeling of tightness and constriction. But being too minimalist with grey and black tones that suggest a spiritual, Zen-like atmosphere is also much too yin. If you are keen on the minimalist look, also introduce yang features to create balance, such as sound and light sources.

Dining room furniture

Comfort is an important consideration at the dining table. Uncomfortable chairs here suggest difficulty in sustaining your present lifestyle. Chairs that are too small for you limit your growth and upward mobility, so choose chairs that are larger rather than smaller. Dining tables that are too small or too narrow again suggest that your success and good fortune cannot be sustained. Eight-sided Pa Kua-shaped tables are regarded as auspicious, but large round tables are best.

Living room furniture

Even if you like the modern Italian designer look, as I do, you really must also use at least one set of chairs with back rests. I keep mine in the room where I meet guests, so that I have a chair to sit on that gives me support. My living room furniture has little back

LEFT Round dining tables and high backed chairs are auspicious dining room furniture.

support and is basically for display, so I do not spend much time here. In my family room, the sofa is lush and very supportive for family members.

Bedroom furniture

Beds must also have support, so a bed head is important. There should never be shelves behind or above you. Your bed must never be too small or too short for you. This constricts your growth and is especially harmful for growing children. Never put two single beds together to become a double bed, or have two mattresses on one bed frame – this will create an invisible line of separation between a couple. It is better to sleep on two separate large beds.

117

COLOUR AND COLOUR COMBINATIONS

The Pa Kua illustrated below shows the correlation between directions and colours. From this we can see, for example, that the south parts of the home and rooms are of the fire element. So, in south corners, red is the complementing colour and green is the enhancing colour because wood feeds and enhances fire. What would hurt would be blue water, which puts out the fire, or earth, which exhausts the fire.

So for each sector there are auspicious and inauspicious colours. There are also auspicious colour combinations which in the south would be green with red, and also blue with green since water

strengthens the wood that feeds the fire. Blue on its own would not be good, but blue with green would be auspicious.

In the north the element is water, which is enhanced by metal, so white is excellent. Colour combinations that are auspicious would be white with blues, or metallic with blues. Green would be bad because it exhausts the water, and earth destroys it, so yellow is also not a good colour for the north.

In the west and northwest the element is metal, which is enhanced by earth, so yellow is great and yellow with white would be very good. The combination of gold with white or with yellow is also good. Red would be disastrous and blue would exhaust the sector.

In the east and southeast the element is wood, so greens and browns would be auspicious. Blue is also very nourishing and combinations of blue and green would be excellent. Avoid reds and whites or combinations of these colours.

In the southwest and northeast the element is earth and thus the colour is yellow. However, the colour red is also excellent here because fire feeds earth. All the bright vibrant shades of red and orange would work well in these corners. The colours to avoid would be green, which hurts the corner, or white and gold, which exhaust it.

You can use these guidelines on colours according to the Pa Kua to select dominant colours for curtains, carpets, cushions, paintings and other interior decoration items. You will find that by doing this you will be adding tremendously to the balance and harmony of your home interiors.

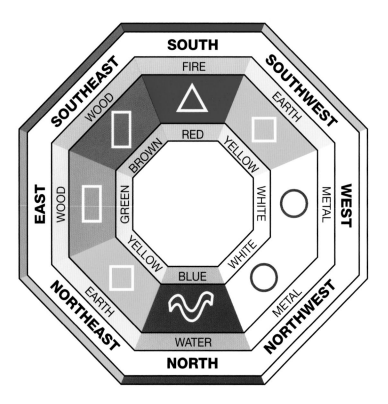

The shapes and colours associated with the elements of each direction

SHAPES AND DIMENSIONS

The shape and dimension of furniture can either add to or detract from the energy of any room, thereby affecting the subtle movements of chi around them. When shapes are in balance and are harmonious to the intrinsic chi of that part of the room and house they occupy, the effect is positive. When they are out of sync, however, the effect is negative.

Shapes

In the illustration shown here, the Pa Kua is superimposed over each individual room. If it was superimposed over the whole house we would know the dominant element of each room as a whole, as well as the individual corners of each room. Since the house faces south, we know that the master bedroom, for instance, is located in the southwest, making the dominant

element here the earth element. This bedroom thus benefits from fire energy, which enhances earth. So triangular-shaped objects, lights and red carpets and curtains would enhance the luck of this room. Too much red, though, would be excessively yang, so it is better to enhance only the southwest corner of the room. A triangular cabinet in that corner is thus auspicious.

Dimensions

In addition to shapes and colours, it is also possible to use a feng shui measuring tape to have furniture made in auspicious dimensions. Go to a specialist feng shui supplier to purchase the measuring tape.

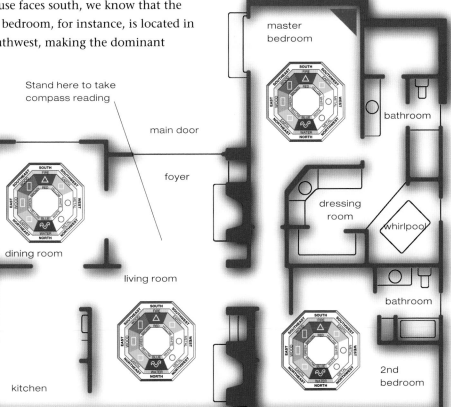

LEFT Colours and shapes should complement the directions of each room or corner. Memorize these complementary attributes to aid your feng shui planning.

USING PERSONAL ELEMENTS

As well as using the Pa Kua direction elements to enhance your feng shui, you can also use your personal element to great advantage.

ABOVE A room adorned with plants will enhance people who benefit from the wood element.

branch element according to your zodiac sign. The objects in your living space should always strengthen this element. Check your zodiac sign on pages 24–25 and then use the information below to check your personal element.

ZODIAC ANIMALS AND ELEMENTS	
Rat – Water	**Horse** – Fire
Ox – Earth	**Sheep** – Earth
Tiger – Wood	**Monkey** – Metal
Rabbit – Wood	**Rooster** – Metal
Dragon – Earth	**Dog** – Earth
Snake – Fire	**Pig** – Water

Many people get confused when it comes to identifying their personal element and this is understandable, because every person is influenced by more than one of the five elements. Based on your birth details it is possible to generate the different elements based on the year, date, month and hour of your birth.

The above creates the basket of elements generated from what astrologers refer to as your Paht Chee chart, or eight characters chart, which enables fortune-tellers to read your destiny luck cycles in conjunction with Purple Star astrology. However, the element to use when planning your personal feng shui is the year earthly

Use your element to get the best luck chi from the furniture around you and especially from your bed and the sleeping area. Do remember that personalizing element enhancement should really only be limited to your bedroom if there are other residents in the home.

Kua numbers

You can use your personal element as defined by the Kua formula (see page 59–60) to apply to beds and bedroom furniture. It is especially potent to apply the personal element to personal adornments such as the colour of clothes, jewellery and face make-up colours and styles.

FENG SHUI IN THE BEDROOM

Feng shui offers a great number of guidelines and lots of advice for the bedroom. There are also many bedroom taboos of which to take note.

These taboos must be observed and taken into account, but a good sleeping direction contributes substantially to your good fortune. The auspicious sleeping direction is where the top of the head points, because chi enters a sleeping person through the crown chakra, which lies at the top of the head. The ability to sleep with your head pointing in a direction from where good fortune comes is a great advantage. So if you want wealth and financial success, you would benefit enormously if you had a bedroom in the house that corresponds to your wealth direction, and placed your bed in the auspicious sleeping direction to enable you to tap your wealth direction while you

sleep. By doing this you will have tapped the double goodness effect. However, in reality, it is not always possible to achieve perfect feng shui. In the illustration, the master bedroom is in the northwest part of the house. In terms of location, this bedroom is beneficial for a west group person. If that person's Kua number is 6, then northwest is his best direction for personal growth, so it is acceptable for the west group person even though it is not the wealth direction. Since the bed is pointing west, it is his wealth direction. This master bedroom is not good for an east group Kua person, although the bed can be rearranged to let the head face north, which is an east group direction.

BELOW This bedroom and bed are excellent for a person with Kua number 6. If it is used by the patriarch, then this location is doubly good since northwest is the direction of the patriarch.

BEDROOM TABOOS

- Do not let the bed 'float' in the middle of the room. There must be a solid wall behind the bed, otherwise your sleep is unbalanced.

- Do not let your feet point directly at the door, as this is the death position.

- Do not let any mirrors face the bed directly.

- Do not have the bed share a wall with a toilet. This causes chi to be afflicted before entering your head.

- Try not to sleep with a window behind you.

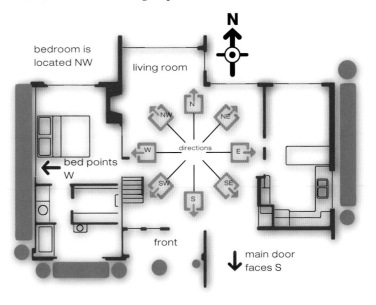

bedroom is located NW · living room · bed points W · directions · front · main door faces S

BEDROOM FURNITURE

Canopy beds are excellent as they suggest a sheltering and protective shield for your sleeping hours. A full canopy is better than a half canopy. Beds should also have headboards and, whatever the design, they should be solid enough to provide good sleeping support. I find that having the wonderful longevity symbol carved onto beds is excellent for health.

Never place beds floating in the middle of the room. I have discovered this to be harmful, causing imbalance and uncertainty. I tried this at the advice of a feng shui master who was an expert in Eight Mansions. His view was to tap the personal sheng chi direction at all costs and I discovered that, despite sleeping in my sheng chi direction, if the bed does not have a solid wall or at least a window (which must be closed with curtains at night), the effect was really not good at all. So, better to sleep with your head facing a less auspicious direction but have support behind your head. Auspicious beds always have good support behind and should not be afflicted by open-shelved bookcases nearby.

COMPATIBILITY WITH YOUR ZODIAC SIGN

Use the productive cycle (see pages 20–21) to obtain the most auspicious type of bed for your personal element.

Snake and **horse** belong to the fire element. Wooden beds are excellent for fire people. Their chi is exhausted if they sleep on a low bed on a cement floor, as cement represents earth energy. They should also never sleep on water beds.

Dog, **dragon**, **ox** and **sheep** belong to the earth element. Anything red benefits earth people. Their chi is exhausted if they sleep on wooden floors, and they should also avoid brass beds.

Pig and **rat** belong to the water element. Water people benefit from brass beds, but they should avoid too much wooden furniture.

Tiger and **rabbit** belong to the wood element. Water beds are destabilizing, so wood people can symbolize water with blue sheets and duvet covers. They should avoid having fire energy – for example, red sheets will sap their energy.

Monkey and **rooster** belong to the metal element. Metal people should always have white sheets. Water beds would be very harmful.

AUSPICIOUS BEDROOM CHIC

You can design very chic-looking bedrooms and still follow feng shui principles at the same time. As long as you position the bed auspiciously according to your lucky Kua directions, while observing the basic guidelines on bedroom feng shui, you will not go far wrong.

Here are some additional tips you will find useful when planning your bedroom.

■ Keep the bedroom regular in shape. No matter how chic an irregular shape may look to you, resist the temptation of agreeing to an L-shaped, U-shaped or triangular-shaped bedroom. Regular size and shape bring better luck.

■ Keep plants and flowers out of the bedroom, as plants here sap your energy.

■ Make sure your bed is not too small or excessively large. Beds that are too small will cramp your growth and development, while beds that are too large can cause relationship problems.

■ Stay clear of abstract designs with arrows and triangles; these represent the fire element, which is bad for the bedroom, and symbolize poison arrows attacking you while you sleep.

■ Use soft pastels rather than loud primary colours. A bedroom dominated by red is suitable for young people, but red is a very yang colour, which is not very conducive to rest. Dark red or maroon is preferable to bright red.

■ Keep wealth and other deities, as well as the celestial creatures, out of the bedroom. It is not advisable to energize the bedroom with feng shui symbols of good fortune, and definitely the dragon should be kept out of the bedroom.

BELOW It is not a good idea to sleep with a window behind you since it suggests no support. Also it is better not to have flowers in your bedroom. In this location, they can sap your energy.

KITCHEN FENG SHUI

According to the Kua formula, kitchens should ideally be located in one of the four bad directions of the family patriarch and should be used to 'press down' on bad luck.

This is based on the premise that the powerful energy produced by cooking is often so strong that it will press down on the luck of its location. It is much better for the kitchen to press down on the patriarch's bad locations than his good locations. Even if the matriarch is the family breadwinner, the kitchen should press down on the bad luck direction of the patriarch. However, the facing direction of the cooking stove should be one of his best directions.

So, take note:

◾ If the kitchen is located in your personal wealth (sheng chi) direction, the result is unpopularity, miscarriages and lack of livelihood. The kitchen will press down on your success luck.

◾ If the kitchen is located in your health (tien yi) direction, you will often get sick and become easily exhausted and weak. The kitchen will absorb all your energy and vibrant chi.

◾ If the kitchen is in the five ghosts (lui shar) direction, you will avoid getting sick and will have success.

◾ If the kitchen is in your romance (nien yen) direction, you will find it hard to get married, and if already married there will be misunderstandings and quarrels. The strong, excessively yang fire energy burns rather than nurtures your relationships.

◾ If the kitchen is located in your personal growth (fu wei) direction, you will be forever poor. You stagnate and live in a continuous state of dissatisfaction. This is potentially the most harmful situation as it cuts directly into your sense of happiness and achievement.

◾ However, in your total loss (cheuh ming) direction, the kitchen will press down all your bad luck associated with this direction. You will have good health.

◾ If the kitchen is in your six killings (wu kwei) location, your family will enjoy steady luck. All bad luck dissipates easily and you escape misfortunes.

◾ Kitchens located in the bad luck (ho hai) direction protect you from losing money and from being cheated by people. You will also have stronger resistance to illness.

You must never place a kitchen in the northwest of the home. If your kitchen is located here, try to relocate it. If you cannot make this change then alleviate the dangerous feng shui by placing a large urn (45cm/8in deep and 30cm/12in across) of still (yin) water in the kitchen. It overcomes the fire energy created by the kitchen.

LEFT Kitchens should be airy and well-lit and kept free of clutter. A kitchen should not be positioned in the northwest part of the house.

GUIDELINES FOR KITCHENS

- You must position the cooker such that the 'mouth' (which I interpret as the oven door, as this corresponds to the concept of the door of the home being the mouth of the home) faces one of the patriarch's four best directions.

- The sink should not confront the stove, since this pits water against fire, representing a clash of elements.

- Similarly, the refrigerator and dishwasher should be placed away from the stove.

- The actual cooking area should not be in the northwest part of the kitchen since this represents 'fire at heaven's gate'.

- All shelves should be closed with doors, which can be glass, wood or plastic.

- Colour schemes should harmonize with the element of the kitchen's location direction.

- White kitchens are excellent if they are located in the west. Kitchens here should not have a red colour scheme.

- Yellow kitchens should be in the earth corners northeast or southwest. Here, avoid using a colour scheme dominated by green or blue.

- North-located kitchens can be in blue, or in black and white, but not in yellow, beige or cream.

- Kitchens in the east and southeast would benefit from a green-dominated colour scheme, but should not be in red or white.

- Kitchens in the south should not be in red, even though this is a fire-element location. Better colours to use are pink or beige, as red in the kitchen is a danger colour, signifying excessive fire energy.

- Always use tiles for the kitchen floor, as this gives it excellent grounding energy. Do not use wood, carpets or linoleum. Kitchens that have windows are better than kitchens that do not. Never allow odours to get too strong and, most important, do not clutter up your kitchen with left-over food.

DINING AUSPICIOUSLY

The Kua formula of auspicious directions can be applied in the dining room to benefit all members of the family. Use a compass to check the direction that each place setting will be facing and then allocate that place to one member of the family.

There is greater flexibility of directions if you use an eight-sided Pa Kua table, but you can use any kind of dining table, and round tables are said to be very auspicious. Square and rectangular tables are also acceptable from a feng shui viewpoint, although being four-sided such tables can sometimes prove to be awkward for tapping auspicious directions. Also, if you have a rectangular dining table, make sure that no one sits at the corners. Never eat with the corner pointed directly at your stomach as this is very inauspicious. The operative direction is the direction you are facing as you sit down to eat.

BELOW Mirrors in the dining room double the food on the table and so create a sense of abundance. Chandeliers bring positive yang chi into the room.

Sit facing your best direction at the dining room table

So if the direction south is good for you, then sit in the place that allows you to face south. The direction you choose as your dining direction need not always be your wealth direction. I prefer to sit facing my family/romance direction, and I also place all members of my family in their respective family/romance directions. This augurs well for the harmony of the family since this direction is also the nurturing matriarchal energy direction. When you eat together facing your respective nien yen directions, there will be fewer quarrels at the dinner table.

When all are facing their wealth/success directions, the amount of aggressive yang energy generated can sometimes cause heated arguments to arise. It is of course understood that you really should not eat

facing one of your four bad directions, especially your total loss (cheuh ming) direction. Doing so brings enormous bad luck indeed. As well as tapping into your good direction, also follow some of the basic feng shui ground rules about the dining room. Here is a quick checklist for you to go through:

■ Try not to have the toilet opening off or sharing any wall of the dining room. If there is a toilet, keep the door closed all the time. The foul energy coming out from there is harmful.

■ Have a wall mirror to reflect the food on the table as this doubles your good fortune.

■ Do not eat directly under a toilet on the upper floor above your table. Really bad luck!

■ Do not eat in the basement or lowest part of the home.

■ Have the dining room deeper into the home. If you eat too near the front door, your wealth tends to seep out.

In the dining room illustrated above, notice how the brightness of the room is supplemented with a good colour scheme. In feng shui almost all shades of all colours (except maybe the darker colours) can be used depending on where the dining room is located. The excellent mirror in the living room also enhances the feng shui of the dining area. This is because there are no dividers between dining and living room space. This is acceptable in feng shui. In the same way the chandelier which hangs in the living room also benefits the dining area.

Note the single column in the right side of the room between the dining and living areas. If you have such a column in your home interior it does not do any harm unless it appears threatening. If you have thicker columns in the home one way of treating them would be to cover them with mirrors.

ABOVE Rectangular tables are better than oval tables, but never sit at a corner. A feeling of space is also good for the flow of chi.

DESIGNING A FENG SHUI DINING ROOM

area on the higher level. But you should not designate a mezzanine floor as the dining room – this halfway floor is very unlucky. Finally, try not to have protruding corners or exposed overhead beams in the dining area. Being hit by poison arrows as you eat is the surest way of contracting serious illness. Should there be exposed corners or square pillars sending poison arrows to the dining table occupants, diffuse the edge of the corner and disarm the poison arrow with plants, by hanging a faceted crystal from the ceiling directly above the edge, or by hanging a wind chime there.

When building a new home, make an effort to design good feng shui in the dining room. In terms of layout, place the dining area at, or very near to, the centre of the house, as this represents the heart of the home. The more spacious the dining room, the better the luck of the family will be. There should ideally be one solid wall in this room, which should be behind where either the father or mother sits. Dining rooms that are part of living rooms are excellent, as this increases the feeling of space. This would be even better if the Flying Star charts indicate good 'numbers' in the centre of the home.

Kitchens placed next to the dining area should be level with or below the level of the dining room. Never have the dining room in a sunken part of the home. If your house has a split level, place the dining

THE EFFECTS OF POISON ARROWS IN THE DINING ROOM

The effects of poison arrows from different directions are as follows:

Southwest will cause womb and stomach problems, such indigestion and miscarriage.

North affect your kidneys and ears.

East result in illness associated with the lungs and feet.

Northwest give you headaches and severe migraine.

West cause lung problems and danger to the head.

Northeast cause back problems and vulnerability to accidents affecting the hands and fingers.

Southeast cause illness associated with the thighs, the buttocks and also cause you to be easily susceptible to flu and colds.

South cause heart and eye problems.

CORRECTING NEGATIVE CHI IN THE DINING ROOM

- Place a potted plant in front of the sharp edges of any protruding corner or column.

- Move the dining table out from under exposed overhead beams.

- Overcome the heavy energy from exposed overhead beams by placing a pair of bamboo flutes in the shape of an 'A' over the edge of the beam.

- Place curtains or blinds at windows to disguise ugly views.

- Protect the dining area from excessive glare from the western sun.

- Check the Flying Star natal chart numbers of the dining area and use element therapy to overcome the effect of bad number combinations in the chart.

ENHANCING THE FENG SHUI

Place a set of the Fuk Luk Sau or the Star Gods in the dining room. Try to buy the best you can afford. These images really are important in this part of the home. The Chinese believe that Fuk Luk Sau encompass all the aspirations of mankind, and their image inside the home does attract a great deal of good fortune. In many Hong Kong homes, I see fabulous versions of this very auspicious symbol of good fortune made of jade, carved out of precious aventurine and some even engraved with real diamonds and gold.

You can also place a symbol of longevity in the dining room area. Since there are many different symbols you can select one that particularly appeals to you – a peach plant rendered in jadeite, an image of the God of Longevity or perhaps an antique urn with images of cranes, bamboo or pine trees.

To attract abundance, hang a painting that symbolizes an abundance of food, a harvesting of a successful crop or other suggestions of plenty. Never hang paintings of animals, abstract patterns or unhappy-looking faces in the dining area. This should be a joyous room where the family interacts happily with each other, so use the walls to create auspicious vibrations.

BELOW
Place images of Fuk Luk Sau in your dining room to enhance wealth luck.

LIVING ROOM FENG SHUI

Your living room is the 'face' you show the world. This is the part of the home most frequently visited by outsiders, so this is the public area of your house. Living room areas should be spacious, and it is a good idea to keep living areas of the home well lit to keep the chi moving.

ABOVE The solid sofa and armchairs make this a supportive living room. However the large plant on the coffee table and square motifs on the floor dominate the room. A sense of balance is important in feng shui.

The furniture should be comfortable and non-threatening – comfortable leather sofas that have good shoulder rests and solid support behind are excellent feng shui, as are fabric sofas.

The living room is probably the best room in the home to decorate with auspicious objects and good fortune symbols, since this is the room you see as soon as you enter the home. A painting of the Eight Immortals, who are revered as Taoist saints, is very auspicious when hung in the living room. The Chinese believe that images of the Immortals in any home bring in the eight types of luck. Most paintings also contain the symbols of good fortune carried by each Immortal, such as the crane, the red bats, the pine tree, the peach, the fan, the wu lou (the symbol of good health) and the fly whisk.

Other good ideas are to place a pi yao, the celestial creature said to have the power to appease the Grand Duke Jupiter, in the centre of the coffee table and to place a tribute horse being pulled in by the God of Wealth on a small side table. On the floor, a large model sailing ship filled with gold ingots sailing in from your most auspicious sheng chi direction is a good idea. A small bowl of growing auspicious bamboo placed on a glass table in the wealth corner of the room is a good energizer.

There is no need to use anything old, antique or Chinese if you do not like this style in your home. I have seen some remarkably beautiful and well-designed modern homes that cleverly incorporate auspicious feng shui principles in the subtlest ways. You can be as modern as you wish.

LIVING ROOM FURNITURE

It is very beneficial to design the furniture arrangements in your living room to create the best feng shui for you according to your Kua directions. You can do this by using colours, pictures, curtains and armchairs that harmonize with the element indicated in your Kua number. You can also focus on the placement of the sofas and chairs so that they face your good directions.

Sofa arrangements and placements should enable you to sit facing your best direction while entertaining your guests. So if your wealth direction is east, then you should arrange the seating such that you can sit facing the east, or at least sit facing one of your four auspicious directions. Better still if you can sit in one of your lucky corners while at the same time facing one of your lucky directions. This brings a double benefit.

However, it is also important to arrange seating in a way that no one sits in the direct 'line of fire' of shar chi, or killing energy, from sharp corners or structural pillars. Where these occur, you can always camouflage them with foliage plants. Pillars can be covered with mirrors – this effectively causes the pillar to disappear visually, thereby not causing feng shui problems. Also, built-in cupboards with exposed shelves will look like blades sending out killing chi – this is not advisable, and the cupboards are best closed up or removed.

LEFT There are no deadly poison arrows in this room. It is spacious, warm and friendly, but the painting of a house above the fireplace is not a good idea and should be removed.

USING ELEMENTS IN THE LIVING ROOM

Using element therapy in the living room is one of the easiest feng shui methods to follow. Go for a productive cycle of colours to create the flow of chi. When selecting sofas and curtains for the living room, you can give your creativity a free rein. But it is also a good idea to consider the distribution of the chi in this room according to the five elements and their associated colours – east and southeast are wood (green), south is fire (red), west and northwest are metal (white), southwest and northeast are earth (yellow), while north is water (blue or black). Applying elements and colours will help you create wonderful feng shui.

An east-sector living room

A living room located in the east of the house will benefit from a preponderance of wood. This will create great harmony in this room. The colour green is also beneficial and you should always have a display of flowers in this part of the home, since flowers in bloom in the east indicate the successful fruition of projects and enterprises. Wood corners also benefit from things that suggest the water element, so using blue curtains or a blue carpet will be very beneficial.

Enhancing a north-sector living room

An oil painting of a waterfall placed on the north wall of the room signifies water coming from the north, which is very auspicious and will help the wood of this room flourish. This painting will be even more auspicious if the Flying Star chart indicates an auspicious water star for this room. In this way, you can incorporate compass feng shui with symbolic feng shui to improve strongly the feng shui of the room.

Red for the south sector

If the living room is located in the south part of the house, then a preponderance of red will be most beneficial. This does

BELOW Cane furniture is excellent for corners in the east and southeast of the home. Here, the picture window draws in sunlight chi from the garden. This is excellent feng shui.

not mean you need to have so much red here that it overwhelms, but it does mean that red should dominate the colour scheme of the room. In the south-located room shown above, red curtains and red scatter cushions will activate the fire element of the room and anyone spending time here will benefit from this tapping of recognition luck. Those belonging to the east group (that is, with Kua numbers 1, 3, 4 and 9) will enjoy a double benefit when they spend time in this room. Note the pink carpets also.

Activating the chi in the southwest

A sofa upholstered in red in a living room located in the southwest of the house (an earth element room) signifies the fire element and since fire produces earth in the cycle of elements, this selection of colours has positive feng shui benefits. The background curtain has an ochre colour, which signifies the earth element. This colour scheme would be less beneficial in a metal element direction (west and northwest) or in a wood element direction (east and southeast).

ABOVE The colours in this room benefit a living room located in the south of the house. However, placement of the furniture where the two sofas directly face each other is very confrontational. You can soften it by placing six crystal balls on the coffee table to enhance relationship harmony.

FENG SHUI ART

Art is something that is extremely personal. Art reflects the mood, the tastes and the attitudes of different people, so it is impossible to say what is good or bad art.

Irrespective of personal tastes, however, it is vital to take a feng shui perspective towards the hanging of art in the home. This is because the chi emanated by hostile images can sometimes be very harmful. Art images can cause misfortunes to occur – and you would not even know why.

The bad luck and misfortune caused by art hanging on walls of homes and offices work quietly and very quickly indeed. I am especially mindful of art that is old or has been hanging in unhappy homes, art that portrays grief, art that features images of ferocious animals, art with dour-looking faces and of grim-looking portraits – the list of potentially harmful art is impossible to quantify. So many aspects come into play – colours, tones, the provenance of the piece and so on. Even images of auspicious objects can be harmful when drawn in an inauspicious way.

For example, take paintings of horses, a popular subject that is also very auspicious. A rearing horse with forelegs raised would be deadly hung behind your chair. An unhappy-looking workhorse creates poverty vibes. And horses with white faces, running in panic, suggest some major disaster is about to happen. Imagine images of such horses in your home!

Many people have asked me about feng shui and art, and I have to say that nothing gives me greater pleasure than visiting art museums in Paris, New York, Saint Petersburg and London. I am a great fan of the Impressionists and love the way they capture sunlight, water and flowers – full of colour and yang energy. They are excellent examples of happy art that create positive vibrations wherever they are hung. But I always wondered at some of the darker, more sombre and unhappy masterpieces of Picasso – would you have a print of his scary Weeping Woman in your home? On the other hand, when you hang prints from his happy 'Blue Period' they are definitely auspicious, as they often indicate a happy family. So the feng shui perspective applies equally well to Western or Eastern art. Look at the colours and symbols – then decide.

Probably the single most powerful art subject to have in your surroundings –

either at work or at home – would be that of mountains. There really is nothing as amazingly supportive as having a beautiful painting of a mountain range behind you – something that can simulate the celestial protective turtle or the powerful yang creature, the dragon. Mountain paintings should be selected with great care. They should look majestic, unshakeable and friendly, and emit a balance of elements that is in sync with the wall on which you plan to hang it.

MOUNTAIN IMAGES GIVE SUPPORT

Mount Everest is an excellent example of a powerful earth element mountain, suitable for walls on the southwest, northeast, west or northwest. Mountains that are lush with vegetation are excellent on walls on the east, south and southeast of your living room. Mountains white with snow are excellent for the east, southeast and north of your home or room. Mountains that look barren or are excessively sharp with lots of triangular sharp peaks would be hostile and are not recommended. Mountains that are yellow, brown and stony-looking, and suggest rocks and granite, would be excellent for the southwest, northeast, northwest and west walls of any room.

Mountain paintings should always show the mountain dominating the valley. If there is a valley in the foreground with the mountains far away, the painting suggests that you will fall over backwards and also that the mountain is subservient to the valley. In feng shui interpretation, this is quite fatal if the painting is hanging behind you. But if such a painting were hung in front of you, it could be auspicious. The idea is to be clear what energy we are tapping.

Mountain paintings should also not have water flows and waterfalls, unless these are so tiny as to be dwarfed by the sheer size of the mountain image itself. This is because when we use mountain energy it must be stronger than water energy.

If you like, you can also use images of holy mountains to give you solid support at work. I am especially fond of this image of Mount Kailash, which Hindus and Buddhists believe is the holy mountain that is the abode of the Gods. Mount Kailash stands solid and powerful among the mountain ranges of the Himalayas on the Tibetan side, and is a place of pilgrimage.

BELOW When selecting mountain images to place behind you, avoid those which also show water. It causes a conflict of symbolism unless the mountain image is placed near the front and is being used to energize an auspicious mountain star 8.

ART THAT BRINGS GOOD LUCK

RIGHT The vibrancy of the play of light and shade on the water in Monet's *Water Lilies* makes it an excellent water energizer.

BELOW Paintings of sailing ships in tranquil waters are always good feng shui since they symbolize the arrival of good fortune.

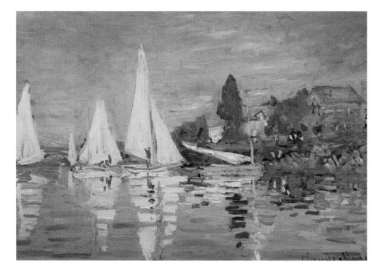

RIGHT This painting by Renoir showing a happy sociable scene, or one like it, placed in the Southwest will bring you many good friends and a full social life.

Illustrated here are three very auspicious Impressionist paintings that would definitely enhance feng shui in the appropriate sector of the home.

This painting by the celebrated artist Claude Monet of sunlight shining on lush growing plants has a wonderful vibrancy and yang energy. The trees look alive and well, so the energy that emanates from a print of this image is sure to be auspicious, bringing growth energy to wood and fire corners. This kind of art would be great for the east, the southeast and the south, but would be unsuitable for the north. This is because these plants would soak up all the water energy of the north, leaving the corner depleted of this vital element.

In this second painting by Monet, the symbol – sailing ships – is already auspicious, for these bring good fortune from the wind and waters. But here we see also beautiful water, blue skies and bright sunshine, all of which are sources of yang energy. Hanging a print like this on the north, the east and the southeast walls would be excellent.

The third painting is by Renoir, another French Impressionist. This is an excellent print to hang in your living room as it brings in the energy of a happy scene. The participants are having a good time socializing on a warm, sunny, lazy afternoon. The meaning, the ambience and the energy created from this image are positive and joyous. During my university days, I hung this print in my room simply because I liked it so much. A feng shui master told me that it also brought me a great social life!

ART THAT BRINGS BAD LUCK

It is just as important to avoid hanging art that will bring bad luck.

Take note of the following:

■ Avoid art that has dark, foreboding colours – the chi created is very yin.

■ Avoid war scenes and fighting – this will cause residents to be confrontational.

■ Avoid portraits of wrinkled old men and women. This creates illness chi.

■ Avoid paintings of fierce animals in the home. Tigers and leopards can turn ferocious.

■ Avoid art that has sharp angular lines suggesting knives and weapons – the chi is killing.

■ Avoid art that depicts silent ghost-like scenery, such as marshlands and forests.

■ Avoid art that shows houses that look haunted, poor or dirty.

■ Finally, avoid old portraits. The Chinese believe that eerie spirits like to make a home hiding behind paintings with faces and especially those with piercingly intense eyes. We cannot be too careful about this …

My horse painting

Many years ago, we decided to have our beloved horse, Justy Boy, painted by a modern Chinese artist. We gave the artist a photograph of my daughter Jennifer leaning on the horse – they both looked

LEFT This painting of an open mouthed, ferocious-looking tiger is very bad feng shui and to be avoided.

smiling and happy. Unknown to us, this excellent artist had a famous trademark – he always included a little cloud in all his paintings, and so he put a cloud just above the horse's head. Shortly after the painting arrived, we hung it in pride of place in our living room.

Justy Boy became lame soon after that and did not recover for several years. One day, I sat in the living room and suddenly noticed the cloud in the painting. I thought maybe I should take the painting down. Believe it or not, that month, after several years of treatment and a lot of money in vet bills, Justy Boy recovered. He is old now and suffers from stiff joints, but at least his lameness is gone. We now keep that painting stored away, and ever since then I have been alert to little details like that.

When I related this experience to an old Taoist feng shui master from Hong Kong, he nodded his head wisely. That was when he told me never to have anything in the home appear as if it is under a cloud. This is not to suggest that clouds are inauspicious – it is only when they seem to be just above you, blocking out the sun.

TRADITIONAL LUCKY SYMBOLS

RIGHT Powerful Fu dogs are excellent for protecting homes. This giant Fu dog guards one of the halls in the Forbidden City in Beijing.

Chinese homes are replete with good fortune symbols decorating art using all kinds of media. Thus our porcelain ware, our Chinese paintings, our sculptures, our dining plates and utensils, our furniture, our screens and room dividers, and just about anything made for the home are decorated with beautiful paintings, carvings and embroidery of all the traditional symbols of good fortune.

I have seen the power of these symbols work so often that I am no longer surprised each time I visit any one of the cities of China and see the enormous influence of auspicious symbols. In the 1980s, when I first visited China, it was the images of the Forbidden City in Beijing that amazed me – gigantic cranes, tortoises, dragons and every kind of good fortune flower. With China opening its doors to the world now, anyone can visit any of its cities and see for themselves the powerful role played by auspicious symbols in the life of the Chinese. Indoors and out, homes and gardens are decorated with traditional auspicious good fortune symbols, the most celestial of which is, of course, the dragon.

It is an excellent idea to offer auspicious symbols as gifts to loved ones. The gift of traditional auspicious symbols is the best – the Laughing Buddha image, for instance, is an excellent offering of happiness vibrations. And it is always a great idea to present peaches, or the God of Longevity, to your parents or grandparents for their birthdays. The gift of longevity is like an amulet, which protects against unnatural death. Always find images that are well-made and decorative enough to add lustre to your home interiors. Never get cheap plastic imitations – the more valuable the medium, the better. Thus symbols fashioned as fine jewellery or made from precious stone carvings are the best.

FOUR SEASONS OF GOOD FORTUNE

Chinese art is always drawn with auspicious decorative symbols. Five red bats around a longevity symbol is popular simply because it attracts such good luck. Likewise, the God of Longevity is a deity that has a place in many homes because it symbolizes good health and long life. The deer, the peach and the bamboo are also auspicious. Here is a list of potentially lucky images for you to consider:

■ Flowers of the four seasons – the chrysanthemum, the plum blossom, the magnolia, the peony and the orchid – all have different nuances of auspicious meanings. It is suggested that homes with young girls always benefit from flower paintings and images, especially those painted with butterflies, since this suggests the presence of many honourable suitors. The peony is the king of flowers in this respect, but the presence of the lotus and water lilies also ensure that young ladies find happy matches. Flowers must never be drawn with thorns – nor should there be any flowers that are faded or wilted.

■ Certain animals in art are especially auspicious – horses, for example, are an excellent subject since they bring recognition, strength, courage and a sense of adventure. Horses should never be running in fear. Frolicking horses with courageous postures are very auspicious. Tribute horses are excellent subjects. Workhorses and injured horses are not auspicious. Other lucky animals featured in feng shui art are deer, elephants and camels, as well as the celestial creatures – the dragon and tortoise.

■ Flower paintings almost always have birds and almost every kind of bird brings good fortune of some kind. The image of birds, or bird feathers, in the car protects against accidents. And a bird picture placed strategically near the door of a house ensures it gets sold as soon as you put it on the market. The phoenix, the peacock and the rooster are three birds associated with feng shui – their images connote a variety of good fortune meanings. A pair of birds, mandarin ducks especially, suggest romance.

LEFT A painting of plum blossom suggests blooms during a time of adversity. It symbolizes resilience and young yang energy combining favourably with aging yang wisdom.

TRADITIONAL CHINESE ART

There are simply so many auspicious images depicted in traditional Chinese art that it is really no problem at all finding suitable art that brings good fortune to decorate the home. But finding traditional Chinese art that can blend into modern homes can pose a challenge to the interior designers. My advice is to go with your own instincts. There are many auspicious images to choose from, so unless you like a piece of art you should not hang it in your house.

Look at this amazing painting of Kuan Kung, the Military God of Wealth, which is so excellent for anyone in business.

I commissioned this piece from an up-and-coming artist from China after searching for many months for someone suitable. You can see why I am so taken with the result – the painting is simply oozing with abundance. It is painted with so many symbolic objects of good fortune that any home would benefit from its presence and its energy. The Military God of Wealth is excellent for business people as it helps them overtake the competition.

It is really easy to find good auspicious art in traditional Chinese paintings as the Chinese are very particular about what they display. Artists who attend art school are usually trained in the symbolism of objects, animals, flowers, birds, fish and so forth. But if you wish to be more discerning, do look for art that displays a strength of chi. This is displayed in the way the brush strokes are executed. When you see a display of good brush strokes or art that is accompanied with good calligraphy then the value of the feng shui meaning is also considerably enhanced.

PAINTINGS THAT ATTRACT WEALTH

Another painting by the same artist depicts the legend of the three-legged toad. This is a universal favourite among business people familiar with the wealth-attracting symbolism of this humble creature. Here coins symbolize gold and it is used to flush out the toad that is said to be the wife of one of the Eight Immortals who was punished for stealing the Peach of Immortality.

The legend of the three-legged toad has made this a universal favourite among many wealth symbols. The Chinese believe that simply placing this creature in the home will attract moneymaking opportunities.

Place this painting in the living room, and the toads under sofas and on low shelves looking at the door, but not directly in front of the main door.

Kuan Kung

Feng shui enthusiasts are agreed that the most popular and universally acknowledged deity of protection to have in the home and office is the image of Kuan Kung, who is simultaneously the God of War and the God of Wealth. The police and the triads in Hong Kong look to this powerful deity for protection, and businessmen engaged in corporate takeover deals always have his image nearby to assure themselves of victory in the highly competitive field of business.

Politicians also believe in Kuan Kung. Merely having his image in the office, especially when placed strategically behind you, would ensure the retention of power and status.

It is believed that Kuan Kung depicted with the nine dragons is an even more

auspicious and powerful image. The Kuan Kung you choose to display should depend on what kind of luck you wish to symbolize. If you like, you can also use a painting of a Western attired general shown looking victorious. Or you can look for a triumphant horse-racing scene that shows a horse winning a race. The idea is to symbolize victory in the face of competition. This will help you to overcome any obstacles to prosperity that you may face.

LEFT Here is a painting that shows the three-legged toad being enticed out to attract wealth for the home. This is a famous painting to place in the home for prosperity luck.

OPPOSITE Shown on the opposite page is Kuan Kung looking majestically triumphant. The Chinese are especially fond of Kuan Kung as he personifies victory in business competition.

141

ART TO ATTRACT ROMANCE LUCK

ABOVE Gustav Klimt's famous painting *The Kiss* is an excellent image to use to attract love, especially when hung in the bedroom.

If you want to attract love and romance into your life, hang romantic art in your home. You can go with the traditional images of mandarin ducks, double happiness, the dragon and the phoenix images, or you can opt for something less esoteric and less Chinese and go Western.

There are many stunningly romantic art pieces painted by legends such as Austrian artist Gustav Klimt. His painting called *The Kiss*, reproduced here, is probably the most universally acknowledged painting of love. Hang this print in your bedroom. There are also other very beautiful European sculptures and paintings that send out some very powerful love vibrations.

Always hang the symbol of love in the corner that benefits romance, which is the southwest corner of the bedroom or the living room.

You can also use two other alternatives:

1 Your nien yen direction according to the Eight Mansions formula, because this is your personal romance direction; or

2 The direction that indicates your status in the family. This means the southeast if you are the eldest or only daughter, the west if you are the youngest daughter and the south if you are the middle daughter. For boys it means the east if you are the eldest son, the northeast if you are the youngest son and the north if you are the middle son.

You may, if you so wish, activate all the walls and rooms of your home that directly benefit your love life. Do this if you are very desperate to find someone; but if you are this desperate, then I do strongly suggest that you get the double happiness image, the pair of mandarin ducks image or the dragon/phoenix image either as a piece of jewellery to wear or as a cloisonné decorative piece to hang on your romance wall, or placed beside your bed.

Remove all animal or people images that show aloneness. By keeping things in pairs you will attract the chi energy of a couple. If you are a woman, look for some male images, and if you are a man, display some female images. It is really important to balance out the yin and yang energy in the home if you want to attract a spouse.

ART IN CHILDREN'S BEDROOMS

The best art to hang in children's bedrooms would be that related to their studies, the acquisition of living skills, and images that attract recognition of their efforts. This means that children's rooms should have images and feng shui enhancers that help them to gain excellent examination results and major scholastic honours. Thus images of the dragon gate – showing the carp jumping over dragon gate (see page 55), three carps holding a crystal globe or the fisherman teaching a young boy how to make a living – are all suitable art and images for a child's bedroom. The fisherman has always been a great favourite with the Chinese, who like to display decorative images.

The painting of a fisherman shown here is ideal in a young child's bedroom. The meaning is both simple and profound – simple in the concept of making a living, profound in that learning is always superior to being spoon-fed.

Young sons also benefit from having a happy horse painting. The horse is a symbol of courage, speed and perseverance and represents the youthful exuberance and adventurous courage of your young son. The colour of the horse has meaning in feng shui. A white horse signifies joyousness as well as leadership qualities. Black horses spell wealth and chestnut-coloured horses signify recognition.

When looking at horse paintings, always select horses with brave-looking expressions. Never hang paintings of horses that look frightened or seem to be running away from an enemy. Frolicking horses are happy horses, but stampeding horses are frightened horses.

The images that you hang in children's rooms should emanate confidence and courage and thus act as a constant inspiration to them in all their efforts.

LEFT In children's bedrooms it is best not to hang posters of war weapons, wild animals or scary creatures, even if they are just cinema posters. Art with a message that children can learn from is best. This picture of a man fishing suggests learning a skill and earning a living.

143

DEALING WITH INAUSPICIOUS CHI

Homes have a subtle, intangible energy caused by influences such as the inner spirit of the home, its hidden history, the lingering energy left over from earlier residents, or simply the inherent earth energy of the space on which the home was built. Sometimes, homes are afflicted with the energy brought by spiritual entities transcended from other realms. When the chi is positive and healthy it brings good luck. When it becomes negative, sick, stagnant or stale, it brings bad luck and disasters. Negative chi creates obstacles that impede the harmonious flow of chi.

Negative chi can be caused by any number of factors. Homes that suffer from years of neglect and are dirty and cluttered contain negative chi. Homes that have seen illness, loss, unhappiness, violence, anger and suicide suffer from the lingering energy left behind by these negative life situations. Negative chi must be cleared, cleansed and purified.

This chapter deals with negative, inauspicious chi. Regular space clearing creates powerful healing energy where there may have been illness, builds stunning harmony where there may have been discord and reintroduces a fabulous new-found strength where there has been weakness. Bad luck stops and good luck flows unimpeded back into the home.

NEGATIVE CHI FROM NEIGHBOURS

BELOW This living area has a round mirror, which reflects another room. Always be careful about using mirrors. Make sure a mirror never reflects a neighbour's house when the neighbour is unfriendly, since this draws in hostile chi.

Unfortunately, negative chi can come from neighbours. When neighbours are friendly, their energy is reinforcing. When vibes are hostile, however, the energy can be harmful. When neighbours send intimidating chi on a regular basis you are sure to succumb unless you tune in to it, recognize it for what it is and do something to dissolve it.

Hostile but harmless chi in the form of frivolous gossip and small-time envy can easily be dissipated by using your own stronger energy to ignore it. If the chi is simply annoying, such as when your neighbour has a house full of screaming children who disturb your rest or break your things, just place a large urn of still (yin) water to the side of your house. The urn should have a wide mouth and a narrow bottom. Place a light inside the water and try to create life as well, with a plant or a few small fish, to bring in yang energy. This will effectively soak in all annoying loud noises and create an invisible absorbing vehicle.

When the energy being sent your way is full of poisonous jealousy, hatred or spiteful gossip, you might want to consider countering with stronger measures. An excellent way to protect yourself from being harmed by this kind of hatred-motivated killing energy is to use a round mirror to reflect back everything negative that is being sent to you. However make sure that it doesn't actually reflect a hostile neighbour's house.

ENERGY FROM PREVIOUS RESIDENTS

Before buying or renting any residential property, do ask about the background and history of previous occupants. Negative chi tends to linger unless cleansed and dissipated.

Negative chi can be left over from occupants whose lives were consumed by anger, bitterness and violence – these strong emotions sometimes get so stuck that no amount of scraping and repainting can remove them. Terminal sickness also tends to generate very sticky chi. The walls and floors and ceiling contain left-over unhappiness and pain, which must be cleared.

Fortunately, there are purification techniques and cures for space clearing, including the use of metal objects such as bells, cymbals and singing bowls to create sounds that absorb the negative chi. The harmonics of metal on metal can be very powerful. The best ones are those made from seven types of metals to represent the seven chakras of the human body and the seven planets that affect the energy of our world.

Using the space-clearing bell is probably the easiest way to lift energy. These are usually handmade and come with a wooden mallet, or with a ringer inside. Ring the bell in a rhythmic way so that the clarity of harmonics is heard, and walk around the rooms three times in a clockwise direction. As you ring, the sound becomes clearer and purer as the energy gets lighter and cleaner. As negative chi dissipates, the sound of the bell will resonate with greater purity.

A singing bowl is even more effective because the negative energy is drawn into the bowl and then transformed into positive chi. The singing bowl has wonderful harmonics and once you get the knack of making it 'sing' you will discover that clearing your space with it on a regular basis does wonders.

Place the singing bowl on a soft cushion in the palm of your hand – this will create better harmonics – and strike the bowl three times to 'awaken' it. Then walk round the room three times in a clockwise direction. Keep striking the bowl, or rubbing the edge with a wooden mallet, allowing the sound to linger as long as possible. You will find that as the energy of the space becomes clearer, the sounds too will become purer.

Singing bowls are hand-made, so each bowl will sound different. You must develop a sense for the singing bowl and tune into its harmonics to see if it has affinity with you. When you find a singing bowl you like and can tune into, do look after it. Never allow the bowl to fall onto a hard surface as this destroys its clearing powers instantly. A bowl you have used over the years becomes increasingly efficient at clearing your space; soon it becomes a trusted and powerful ally of the home.

ABOVE The singing bowl is an excellent way of clearing left-over bad energy. But do note that singing bowls should never be dropped – this will render them flawed for the purpose of space clearing.

147

PROBLEM AREAS

The challenge of feng shui is to be sensitive to structures, such as beams, pillars and protruding corners that might hurt the home interior, and to know how to deal with them.

POISON ARROWS

The occurrence of hostile chi in home interiors usually emanates from protruding corners and exposed overhead beams. Structural beams create the most hostile chi. Do watch out for these in your home; if you have exposed beams, try never to sit under them. In addition, you should not sit in the line of hostile chi coming out from a protruding corner. Also, try arranging your furniture so that beams and corners do not face sitting or sleeping areas. The negative effect usually shows up in illness.

Older and frail people are particularly at risk. Their beds should never be under these features. If you cannot move from under beams, hang bamboo tied with red string or two flutes with the mouth side down in an 'A' configuration to reduce their ill effect.

If you wish to enhance your interior design with beams or decorative lines on the ceiling, incorporate it with auspicious symbolism – for example, by using the auspicious trigram Chien, which comprises three straight lines.

RIGHT A pillar can dominate a room in a negative way. Pillars are best when they flank doorways and entrances but are never auspicious in the centre of the room.

PILLARS AND CORNERS

As a general rule, round pillars are preferred to square pillars. Round pillars signify chi moving upwards and bring the promise of abundance. In modern homes, high round pillars can transform a house into a palace, thereby creating the chi of abundance and prosperity. If you live in an apartment building, the presence of round pillars has the potential to transform your building into an auspicious and abundant abode.

However, it is important never to overdo the presence of these soaring pillars. When there are too many of them, something auspicious can transform into excessive yin energy. There is also the question of balance. If yours is a modest home, make certain the size and height of pillars blend harmoniously. Never allow pillars to dominate your living space or your entrance. When balance goes out of sync, the chi will no longer be in harmony.

MIRROR REFLECTIONS

Mirrors are powerful feng shui tools in that they can do wonders for doubling your wealth, your good fortune and your happiness. But mirrors can also bring havoc into your life when they are inadvertently positioned in the wrong places. Whether mirrors bring good luck or bad depends very much on what they are reflecting. So the mirrors inside your home must never reflect anything that suggests wealth flowing outward or, worse still, bringing danger into the home.

■ Mirrors reflecting the main front door cause wealth and good fortune to come in and then instantly flow out again. This is because the mirror is reflecting the outside of the house each time the door opens.

■ Mirrors reflecting the bed cause the marriage to get crowded. Feng shui masters warn against mirrors doubling the yin energy in the bedroom and creating problems with sleeping. Mirrors that reflect a sleeping couple can cause one of them to

LEFT A mirror that reflects a dining table is said to be beneficial as it reflects food on the table. This is not to be confused with mirrors that reflect food being cooked, which would be inauspicious.

have a sexual liaison outside of the marriage. A mirror inside a bedroom that reflects both the door and the bed is doubly bad.

■ Mirrors reflecting the stove or the cooker are also bad news. I have been warned against this ever since I can remember. It is dangerous to reflect a naked flame as this causes accidents to happen. Reflecting the food being cooked in the kitchen is not the same as reflecting the food being served in the dining room, which is very auspicious.

KITCHEN WOES

Although the kitchen benefits from feng shui treatment, there is no need for you to activate the chi here. What is more important is to observe the feng shui taboos.

These are as follows:

■ Do not hang family portraits, mirrors or fierce animals in the kitchen. The fire energy there is much too strong and if it were to be magnified it could badly afflict members of the family. Animal pictures should not be placed here either, since the animal realm generally offers protector images in feng shui. Setting them near fire causes disturbance of an auric nature within the home and the energy generated in the kitchen can then become harmful.

■ Do not have a colour scheme for the kitchen that is dominated by red. There is already enough fire here and too much can pose a danger. Excessive yang energy always poses a real danger, so turn to pastel colours instead.

■ Try to position the cooking direction in such a way that the cook does not have his/her back to the door. This brings bad luck into the kitchen.

■ Try not to position the kitchen in the centre of the home. Having fire at the heart of the home is never encouraged. If your kitchen is in the centre of the home, try to keep cooking with a naked flame to a minimum. This reduces the danger of fire getting out of control.

RIGHT The use of 'islands' in the kitchen layout is an excellent way to ensure a good flow of chi in the kitchen.

DEALING WITH INAUSPICIOUS CHI

INCONVENIENT TOILETS

Toilets and bathrooms tend to be places where bad chi is created and accumulated. Each of the Pa Kua's eight directions superimposed onto a living space indicates a specific kind of luck which is afflicted if a toilet or bathroom is located there. Hence toilets are a source of problems wherever they are located in the home – these modern conveniences seem to be a real inconvenience when we want to practise feng shui. Take note of these cures and remedies:

LEFT Toilets should never be activated with auspicious symbols of good fortune. Keep toilets small and neat and tidy. Whenever they are located in good luck areas or corners, make an effort to energize the area outside the toilet to counter the bad effect of the toilet.

■ A toilet placed in the south causes harm to your reputation, makes you unpopular, and when compounded by other bad indications can even lead to legal entanglements and imprisonment. Place a jug or urn of yin (still) water in the room to counter this.

■ A toilet in the north afflicts your career and slows down your upward mobility. A plant counters the afflicted chi here.

■ A toilet in the east afflicts your health and limits your growth. Place a red lamp in the toilet or, better yet, hang a tiny curved knife (about 7.5cm/3in) to slice through the afflicted chi.

■ A toilet in the west afflicts your descendants' luck and your children. Place a red lamp or a bowl of yin (still) water to control the bad chi.

■ A toilet in the southwest afflicts marriage and marriage opportunities. Overcome this affliction with a plant or by hanging a five-rod solid wind chime.

■ A toilet in the northeast afflicts education and examination luck. A plant here will take care of the affliction.

■ A toilet in the southeast afflicts your family fortunes, causing loss of wealth. Place a small curved knife or have a bright light in the room.

■ A toilet in the northwest causes loss of patronage luck. It also has a negative effect on the luck of the family patriarch. This is a serious affliction and the best way to overcome it is by having the toilet well lit and by having an urn of water.

It is also unlucky when toilets directly face the main door, or doors into bedrooms and dining rooms. In this situation, hang a wall covering to block the toilet visually. Placing a door mirror on the outside of the toilet door or painting the room a bright red are also good solutions. These strengthen the yang chi. If there is a toilet on the upper floor above the main door, keep the entrance foyer or dining room well lit. This has the effect of pushing the chi upward.

IRREGULAR-SHAPED ROOMS

Square and regular-shaped rooms suggest balanced feng shui and are easy to enhance. Irregular-shaped rooms, on the other hand, present something of a challenge. Not only are such rooms unbalanced and with missing corners, they are also difficult to assess and to enhance. It is difficult to superimpose the Lo Shu square onto irregular-shaped rooms, thus making it hard to make Flying Star feng shui assessments of the space. It is also harder to use the Pa Kua eight directions to identify lucky and unlucky corners according to the various schools of feng shui.

BELOW Triangular-shaped bedrooms pose a challenge. Use furniture to cordon off offending corners, making the room appear more symmetrical.

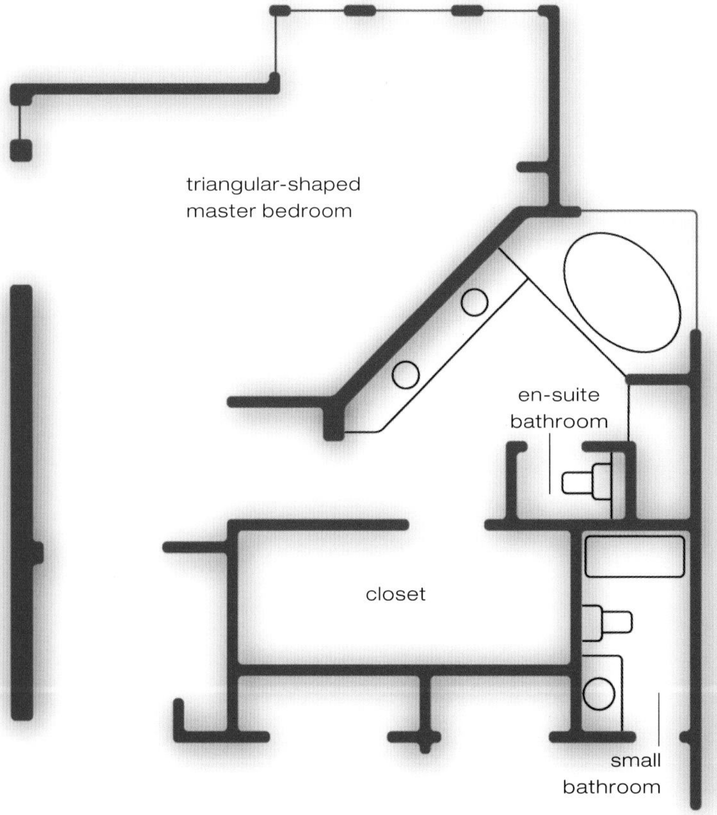

triangular-shaped master bedroom

en-suite bathroom

closet

small bathroom

L-shaped rooms

The most common of irregular-shaped rooms are those that are L-shaped – and these are usually bedrooms that have en suite bathrooms. L-shaped rooms are easy to correct since all that is needed is the placement of some kind of barrier – screen, sideboard or curtain – to create a visual separation. This has the effect of demarcating the sleeping area, which then makes it easy to position the bed and other furniture. If the missing corner of the room houses the bathroom, then introducing the correct cure for the bathroom (see page 151) brings the area back into balance.

Triangular-shaped rooms

In the illustration shown here, the placement of the bed will pose a challenge because of the placement of the two doors into the bedroom. Placing the bed against the wall, which has basins on the other side, will create incredibly bad feng shui for the sleeping residents. Here, the best thing to do is to close one of the doors, perhaps the one leading to the garden terrace, so that the bed can be placed against this wall.

Triangular-shaped rooms are very unsuitable as offices and bedrooms. It would be advisable to look for an alternative room to work or sleep in. If you have no choice, the way to deal with such rooms is to use furniture or curtains to cordon off a corner, which you can use to store clothes, suitcases and so on. This visually and mentally demarcates the area. You can then treat the remaining area as a regular-shaped room.

CRAMPED SPACES AND NARROW CORRIDORS

Two of the most important things to look out for in interior feng shui are dark corners and cramped spaces in the home. This is because stagnant chi accumulates and this creates stale energy that can cause illness, lethargy, fatigue and general apathy. Cramped spaces suggest that life does not flow smoothly. There is little room to move, so chi stagnates. You will feel that there are obstacles to the smooth flow of your life.

Cramped spaces are caused by low ceilings and small rooms. Narrow corridors and tight staircases are also the cause for this affliction. In the layout of an apartment shown here, the corridor that connects the foyer to the bedrooms is too narrow, such that chi will tend to stagnate there unless the corridor is kept brightly lit at all times. Since corridors are conduits of chi, they must not be ignored. It is also a good idea to hang pretty pictures and even a wall mirror to improve the space visually. Narrow staircases can be improved in a similar way.

The best antidotes for cramped spaces are cleanliness, white paint and lights. Take stock of your home and see if there are corners where stagnant chi accumulates. If there are, organize a major cleaning of the space. If a corner feels stale and 'dead', revitalize it with sounds and incense to make the chi come alive again. Then paint it – white is best as this is a very strong yang colour that complements all other colours. Cramped spaces painted white look instantly better – brighter and lighter. The energy improves almost instantly. To ensure that tight spaces never feel cramped, install soft, warm lights that will further improve the flow of energy. Keep these lights turned on all through the day if necessary. The flow of chi will improve.

LEFT Use built-in cupboards to close up small corners. Otherwise stale chi gathers there.

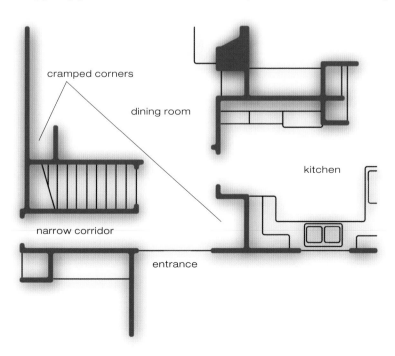

cramped corners

dining room

kitchen

narrow corridor

entrance

STAIRCASE SUGGESTIONS

The staircase in your house or apartment is basically a conduit of chi. It is where chi moves from one level of the home to the next. When your staircase has good feng shui, it distributes good fortune to the rest of the home. When it is flawed from a feng shui perspective, it spreads harmful energy causing illness, robbery and loss. A staircase that conducts afflicted chi is really bad news.

BELOW Staircases are best when they are broadly curved, though they should not resemble a corkscrew.

There are several ways to assess your staircase. Try to incorporate the general guidelines that ensure good staircase feng shui. This requires good staircase design and location. The former is based on the form school, while actual location of the staircase is best assessed according to the Flying Star chart of the home or by using the Pa Kua eight directions.

These are the general ground rules on staircases:

■ Staircases should never face a door. If your staircase directly faces your main front door, place a screen or divider between the stairs and the door. If you cannot do this, try to turn the last three steps of the staircase, and if you cannot do this, then install a very bright and elaborate light fixture in the space between. This will cause the chi entering the house to slow down before making its way up the stairs. A crystal chandelier is best for this purpose. Upstairs the same rule applies. Try not to let the top of the staircase directly face the bedroom door. If it does, once again a bright light here will remedy the situation.

■ Staircases should not have 'holes' in the steps. These suggest a 'leak' in your wealth. Even if you have rented an apartment with this feature, it really is worthwhile to close up the gaps with carpet or plywood. When the staircase looks solid, the flow of chi between house levels is also firm and strong. Note that wooden staircases symbolize growth and are to be favoured.

■ Curved staircases are the best. Broadly curving staircases are the most conducive to an auspicious flow of chi. Spirals are not the same as curved staircases and are not encouraged for indoors, but if you really like a spiral staircase that leads up to a mezzanine floor, use wood rather than metal. Straight and steep staircases cause chi to move too fast. When you have a steep and straight staircase, it is less harmful when placed by the side of the home. When it is in the centre of the home it can be the cause of severe afflictions that result in loss and illness.

STAIRCASE PROTECTION

Staircases that are excessively narrow are best kept lit through the day. Like corridors, staircases are conduits of chi, so it is always a good idea to keep them bright and attractive. In addition, it is also an excellent idea to create staircase protection so that bad energy does not move up the stairs into the sleeping quarters of the home.

■ The best way to ensure this is to hang a picture of a 'protector' image. The Chinese believe in protector images such as Chung Kwei and Kwan Kung. Paintings of these deities can be hung at the base of the stairs to create protective chi here.

■ Another method is to place two small images of Chi Lin or Fu Dogs by either side of the stairs. A third method is to have a very bright light at the base of the stairs so that good luck chi is encouraged and enticed to travel upward.

■ Try not to keep the spaces below the staircase empty. Put this space to good use by converting it into a storage area, but never place things that represent family wealth in this area. Nor should you keep things like text books here since you really do not want to step on anything that symbolizes your own aspirations.

■ Water under the staircase hurts the second generation, so do not place a water feature or a decorative pond under the staircase as this will afflict the success potential of your children.

■ Staircases can be made of wood, metal or concrete to simulate these three solid elements. Use the productive cycle of the five-element theory when choosing your staircase. A wooden staircase works best when it is in the south and metal staircases are best in the north, while concrete staircases work best in the west and northwest.

■ Try not to have staircases in the centre of the home or too near and directly facing the front door.

ABOVE Narrow cramped staircases do not encourage the flow of chi. Wherever possible let your staircase be broad.

WHEN THERE IS ILLNESS ...

According to feng shui, when serious illness strikes it is often because of sickness stars. These can affect young children under the age of 12 or older people of the household, who are weaker and more vulnerable and sensitive to changes in energy. When the family falls ill, the best cures are the metal cure and especially the sound of metal.

Singing bowls create a powerful metallic resonance that is incredibly efficient in absorbing sickness chi in the home. As with space clearing (see page 147) you should walk round the room three times in a clockwise direction, striking at the singing bowl or rubbing its edges with a wooden mallet. This will make the bowl sing and in singing it creates a vibrational force that cleanses the air of sickness chi. Within minutes you will feel the room get lighter and brighter. Illness stars will be considerably weakened.

To take care of sickness-causing Flying Stars you can also hang six-rod metal wind chimes. As we saw on page 94, in the Flying Star system of feng shui there are several number combinations that indicate the presence of illness-causing energy, and for these the metallic wind chime is an effective cure.

As a short-term measure, singing bowls and metal wind chimes are an excellent cure even if you do not know Flying Star feng shui. It is advisable, however, to investigate further and see if you can effect a long-term cure as well. By knowing that illness stars are actually earth element stars, we know to use metallic energy to weaken them.

Another way to control illness stars is to paint the walls pure white. Few people realize the immense power of white. This is the colour of metal but it is also the colour that contains all the seven colours of the rainbow, making it intensely powerful. So when someone is ill, placing him or her in a room with white walls is excellent.

White or blue flowers are also the best to send as a 'get well soon' offering. Refrain from sending red flowers to someone who is ill, and never send red with white, as this is a very unfortunate combination.

RIGHT When sending flowers to someone ill, avoid sending red flowers. Best are white and blue flowers that favour quick recovery.

SUNSHINE WATER CLEARS DEATH VIBES

Where there has been a death in the family, it is very re-energizing to undertake a ritual cleansing with bells and incense. To complete this ritual, it is a good idea to follow it through after the seventh day with a thorough clean using sunshine water.

It is believed that by the seventh day the soul of the person who has passed on will have left the premises and gone on to what is known as the state of bardo – the state between death and rebirth. By the 49th day the soul will have taken rebirth or gone on to pure land. These traditional beliefs are part of the spiritual tradition of China and many other Asian countries. Rituals and practices associated with the three major events of life – births, marriages and deaths – are based on these beliefs. After death there is always symbolic cleansing to aid the departed soul along its way. The space left behind should also be infused with living yang energy to benefit the living.

Sunshine water is water that has been left out in morning sunshine for at least three hours. The Chinese like to keep urns filled with water outdoors to absorb the energy of the sun, the moon, the wind and the air as well as the rain. In modern times, when we get our water from the tap, leaving water out for a while is also a good way for harmful chemicals like chlorine to evaporate. This softens the water considerably and makes it excellent for a variety of purposes.

LEFT Place a container of water in the sun for three hours to soak up the sunshine energy. Cleaning the home with this water will revitalize stagnant energy.

When you clean the home with sunshine water, make sure that the floor is covered with water. However, this applies only to the ground floor of homes. Sunshine-empowered water seeps into the base of the home, revitalizing it and cleansing it of any lingering death energy. If you live in an apartment you cannot do this ritual, as it will be ineffective. In this case, use a damp cloth soaked and rinsed with sunshine water to mop the floor and wipe table tops. This will symbolically regenerate the energy.

PURIFYING WITH FRAGRANT SMOKE

The use of aromas to revitalize spatial energy has been universally accepted by the cultures of many traditions and in recent times this has become popular again.

RIGHT Incense and fragrant smoke have the power to break down negative chi. Use them regularly to cleanse your space.

When you work with energy, you will understand that aromas permeate the consciousness of space. This helps to lighten it, thereby dissolving negative and hostile energy. It is a matter of personal preference what scents you use, but some are more powerful than others.

Sandalwood is particularly uplifting. It is also a very spiritual scent, with its wood revered in China and India. It absorbs negative energy that sticks on surfaces, clothes, walls, floors and even the air itself. It is wonderful to finish spring-cleaning with whiffs of burning sandalwood incense. If you are ill, have a clogged nose or are down with the flu, light a stick of sandalwood incense to feel instantly embraced in an aura of healing energy. Lavender is also very conducive to reducing heaviness in the air. It is said to bring out the creative spirit of our consciousness and is especially wonderful for transcending into other dimensions of consciousness through meditation therapy.

Aromatherapy today blends easily with many feng shui rituals. The release of natural aromas into space through the burning of incense invokes subtle energy fields and it is these that determine the quality of chi in any space. I do believe that fragrance and aromatic oils have tremendous healing power, and anyone can incorporate these into a powerful space-purifying ritual with great success.

When you use incense to create fragrant sacred smoke, begin by generating a quiet mind and a good motivation, which is to keep the energy of the space light, thereby keeping illness and misfortunes at bay. Open doors and windows to bring in new winds, then follow through with the sacred smoke ritual, using fragrant incense or aroma sticks and allowing the smoke to dissipate through the rooms of the home. Use incense-burning saucers and bowls made of metal and decorated with auspicious symbols – such as the protector known as Pi Yao or a lotus-shaped burner. I use the nine dragons to create the chi of courage and strength and the lotus when I want to generate a more refined ambience.

YANG SOUND IS GOOD THERAPY

The energy of homes comes alive instantly when you use sound therapy – the sound of music, people, children, pets, chimes, bells and bowls, drums and cymbals.

Every tradition uses the throbbing and rhythmic sounds of various instruments to breathe yang life into a special day, a celebration or a happy occasion. The Chinese tradition always uses sounds – the sudden burst of firecrackers exploding during the New Year, the beat of drums at festivals to bring in the colourful lions with their yang energy. Bells and cymbals are also extensively used to awaken the chi of spaces. When wealthy people move into their homes they go through the ritual that always includes drumbeats, bells and clashing cymbals. Better yet when there are lions dancing and prancing around!

In your home, the use of sound therapy can be done on a less grand scale. Home energy need not be so powerful. Thus windchimes are an excellent way of capturing natural sounds from the winds. These chimes can be made of metal but they can also be made of bamboo. The sounds emitted are very different. You can use both types – metal for the west and northwest corners and bamboo for the wood corners east and southeast. The reason for this is that the two elements that are being enhanced here – wood, which brings prosperity, and metal, which brings gold and success – are those most commonly associated with material success.

Hang these sound enhancers in the corners of your home, but also bring in the sounds of laughter as often as possible. The yang that comes from happy people is very powerful, so keep inviting your friends over to have a good time. It is far more powerful than you realize. And when you have a shop opening for business, or a wedding, or you are moving into a new home, or simply celebrating the start of a new year, bring on the lions … the combined use of cymbals clashing, drums beating and a few red and gold lions happily prancing around creates an incredibly powerful store of yang chi.

ABOVE During the Chinese New Year celebrations the sounds of cymbals clashing and drumbeats are used to awaken and energize the surrounding chi.

WHEN THERE IS A SERIES OF ACCIDENTS

Negative energy in the home often causes an unrelated yet discernible pattern of accidents – someone banging into your car in the morning; reversing into a drain; hitting your head against a beam; missing your step and falling down.

When you experience a series of small accidents like this happening to you, one of three things can be out of sync in your home:

■ It could be that the annual and monthly Flying Stars have brought some bad luck to your front door or to the bedroom you occupy. It is a good idea to check this out if you can, before something more serious happens. Usually the star numbers 5 and 2, either singly or together, coming into the sector where the front door is located, can cause a whole month's-worth of bad luck. Hang a small six-rod all-metal wind chime near the front door and see if the accidents or illnesses stop. If so, leave it there for about 30 days and then remove it.

■ The entrance of the house has become afflicted with excessive amounts of the element that destroys the element of the main doorway. This affliction may also have occurred in your bedroom. You need to be familiar with the directions of your home and the elements of each part. You will then know if there is a conflict of elements. For example, if you suddenly decide to place a tree in the earth element southwest corner of the house and your front door is located here, the chi of the front door gets sapped. Remove the tree! Everything that happens to your environment affects the chi.

■ The entrance into the house is severely blocked by boxes, newly arrived furniture and so forth, and it has not been moved for various reasons. This can cause a series of misfortunes unless rectified, so never allow unopened boxes to become clutter.

If you cannot find anything that could be causing the accidents, it may be that a family member has inadvertently brought home some 'dirty energy'. You can always use the space-clearing rituals referred to on pages 156–158 and see if this helps to ease the situation. Leave the incense burning each day inside a pi yao – the incense activates this protective creature.

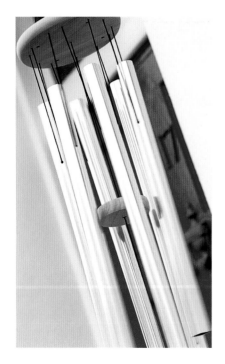

BELOW If you are experiencing a run of accidents, try hanging a small six-rod all-metal wind chime outside your front door.

WHEN RELATIONSHIPS GO WRONG

If things start going wrong for you in your interaction with people at work and socially, you can suspect that something in the energy of your space is having a negative effect on your relationship luck.

This is usually caused by afflicted earth energy in the home, which in turn can be caused by the simple passage of time (so the cause could be bad Flying Stars in your bedroom or around your front door), or the placement of plants in the wrong part of the home. Plants signify wood energy and when these are inadvertently placed in earth corners (southwest and northeast), they deplete the earth energy.

Sometimes you pile junk in spare corners until you can dispose of it. This can trigger off some negative effects and cause feng shui afflictions to manifest. The most vulnerable is when main doorways and bedrooms are affected. So when things suddenly start going wrong, check that nothing is blocking the flow of chi.

If all seems well there, it could be your Flying Stars – to be on the safe side, hang a small metal wind chime near the door and see if things get better. If they do, you are on the right track and hanging another wind chime will strengthen the remedy.

Quarrels and arguments are another way that afflicted feng shui can manifest. When husband and wife start quarrelling for no apparent or logical reason, the cause is usually a bedroom afflicted by a quarrelsome Flying Star number. The most effective remedy is to place something in

LEFT A red and gold object placed in the bedroom will overcome the quarrelsome Flying Star numbers that are causing problems in your relationship.

red and gold in the bedroom. When my family is going through a period of being hostile and confrontational, it is almost always because the quarrelsome star has flown into the dining or family room. I have something red and gold hanging permanently in these rooms. The remedy can take the form of a painting of mandarin ducks and lotuses or goldfish and lotuses, as these signify purity and love; together with the gentle suggestion of yin water, this will appease the quarrelsome star. Also, reduce noise levels in those rooms where the family gathers, as noise will trigger the hostility star.

DISSOLVING TENSION AND ANGER

An excellent way to dissolve tension and anger is by placing six round crystal balls in the family areas of the home, especially in either the southwest or northwest corners. These suggest smoothness in relationships. The number 6 signifies heaven and the crystal balls indicate a union of the heaven and earth trigrams – Chien with Kun.

A large single-pointed natural crystal – placed in the centre of the home with a light shining at it – will reduce all tensions, and any tendency towards anger, violence and hostility will be considerably reduced.

If the problem is continuous anger that leads to violence and loud quarrelling, invest in a vase to apply the yin water cure. The Chinese word for vase is 'ping', which stands for peace, and many Chinese homes display beautiful vases to create an atmosphere of peace and harmony. However, vases only work their potent magic when displayed in homes that are clear of clutter and when they are filled with still (yin) water, which has the power to absorb and dilute anger.

Burglary

Houses suffering the nasty after-shock of being burgled need to be cleansed instantly of the negative energy. When your house has just been burgled, use a mixture of salt and saffron water to cleanse all the doorways and windows of the home. Move three times round the openings in a clockwise direction. Next, place a salt-and-saffron water solution at the entrance of the doorway, leaving it there for three days. Also, keep the lights turned on for at least three days.

Another cure is to use a singing bowl to absorb left-over negative energy. Usually when a home has been burgled, residents live in fear during the following weeks and it is necessary to lift this cloud of apprehension or negative energy, which can act as the catalyst for some other type of misfortune to occur.

An effective antidote to being burgled is an inverted broom placed by the wall next to the door. This is said to ward off the chi of robbery. The Chinese also believe that a pair of Chi Lin or lions flanking the doorway act as a powerful deterrent.

Legal entanglements

Yin water is said to be powerful in absorbing the quarrelsome vibes that lead to legal entanglements. Remove all wind chimes, clocks and other moving objects from the vicinity of the door. Place an image or a figurine of a bird in flight near the door, flying outward – this is believed to reduce the negative impact of legal battles and could even solve the problem altogether. Birds are usually excellent symbols of appeasement and also for warding off accidents. If you are involved in a lawsuit, wear birds fashioned into jewellery, preferably appearing to fly.

Gossip

If you suffer from negative gossip at work and in your social life, the best way to cleanse this negative energy, and reduce its occurrence and its effect on you, is by using sounds to scare away the devil of chatter. Hanging a pair of metal cymbals just inside the home will symbolically override the negative effect of gossip.

You can also wear the mystic knot in green (non-gem-quality jade) to put a stop to idle gossip pertaining to your business, in gold to reduce all frivolous gossip and with diamonds to counter gossip that harms your career. You can also wear coloured crystals to overcome gossip.

Jealousy

The rooster image is the cure for jealousy at work that leads to really harmful gossip. Place a white (or gold and red) rooster on your office desk, and let it peck away all your problems. The rooster cure is especially suitable for those whose desks are placed in tight corners or who are sitting in a 'centipede' arrangement – one desk behind another in two rows, an arrangement that gives rise to the sting of gossip and malicious backbiting.

To ensure that you are adequately protected, place a brass mirror in the home, in the corner diagonal to the main door. The Chinese are also great believers in

wearing amulets and talismans (see page 178). Wearing the dragon, tortoise, Chi Lin or the mystical symbols are excellent for warding off any negative arrows that get sent your way.

Sword coins, made from old Chinese coins tied together with red thread, are said to slice through invisible negative energy with great accuracy, and curved knives made of metal are also effective in clearing the space of negative intangibles that may affect one's well-being.

ABOVE White porcelain vases that have a smooth finish can be a good substitute for crystal balls. The smoothness of the surface creates smooth relationships and the smooth flow of projects by dissolving obstacles.

163

TAOIST FENG SHUI

Taoist feng shui engages the inner chi of mankind, using secret techniques that unite heaven, earth and mankind to create awareness of shifts in the subtle chi. These movements affect our well-being, facilitating direct communication with nature, and with winds and waters. It enables us to read signals from the environment and from the realms of animals, from weather changes, from cloud formations, from signs sent from the cosmos – all seen within the context of time and space.

Inner feng shui engages meditation, breathing and visualizations to infuse the clothes and jewellery we wear with powerful chi, helping us to transform ordinary symbols of nature, from the animal realms and from mysterious past traditions into powerful amulets and talismans, which though fashioned by man are empowered by heaven's blessings.

TUNING IN TO THE UNIVERSE

One of the most exciting dimensions of Taoist feng shui is its focus on the mysterious connections between the human body and the cosmic chi of the Universe. Taoist feng shui is inner feng shui, a set of principles and practices that produce shifts in awareness that improve the way we interact with the environment. The common thread that connects man and his environment is chi, the life force we describe as energy.

Taoist feng shui embraces the whole mysterious world of chi kung, which can be translated to mean the expertise of energy. Chi kung (or qi gong) is the opening of one's body and mind to shifts in chi via physical movements and postures accompanied with breathing and visualizations. At a higher level, meditations become part of the training.

RIGHT This painting depicts the Eight Immortals 'crossing the great waters'. The Eight Immortals personify all the highest manifestations of chi, and having their images in the home symbolizes the ultimate of all good chi.

With years of practice, the reading of and awareness of energy becomes second nature. Chi manifests in ten thousand different ways. Taoist feng shui tunes into chi to understand the workings of the Universe and their manifestations.

It is this awareness that gives rise to an understanding of the environment, of nature and of its effect on the fate of man. This understanding can be so stunning in its veracity that sometimes we think of it as Taoist magic. And this goes back to the shamanic heritage of ancient China. Our cultural traditions and legends are filled with stories of celestial masters who seemed to have amazingly yogic powers – they could fly through the sky, be in several places at one time, appear and disappear at will, and communicate with creatures from different celestial and hell realms. Feng shui really only scratches the surface of Chinese mystical and magical traditions.

Every physical feat that goes beyond ordinary human endurance is attributed to chi. A falling leaf is chi. A child crying is chi. Meeting the man of your dreams is chi. Getting a great job offer is chi. Winning is chi. Losing is chi.

CREATING SEVEN TYPES OF AWARENESS

When there is no chi we are dead. When it is available in abundance, life is a ball. Taoist feng shui focuses exclusively on the chi. Tuning in to the chi, Taoist masters are able to read signals from nature, and understand the signs that reveal things to us about forthcoming events, people and situations. These signs also reveal when the chi needs replenishing and when chi has turned bad.

Taoist feng shui takes us into another realm of space enhancement – one that engages the mind at inner levels, one that with training enables us to use our body centres as sensors. These engage the seven types of awareness that reflect the seven energy centres of the body.

The development of awareness at these levels is not the same as the seven energy centres of the chakra system. According to the Chinese, the energy source is at the centre of the body situated just below the navel. Energy flows through the body via the vertical axis and the meridians, and a field of energy is created. Taoist masters speak of solar chi kung and lunar chi kung.

Solar chi kung uses the sun energy to activate the nine orifices of the body to an awareness of energy, and doing this successfully is said to be excellent for improving health and mental clarity. It also detoxifies the body and contributes to the build-up of a strong immune system. Lunar chi kung uses moon energy to balance the two vertical axes of the body. This method regulates the internal flow of fluids and opens up the five psychic channels of the body.

To learn the correct physical exercises, breathing, and ultimately meditations and visualizations, you will need to find a well-qualified chi kung master.

LEFT A series of slow exercise movements that move the chi within the body, known as chi kung, are integral to developing the seven types of awareness.

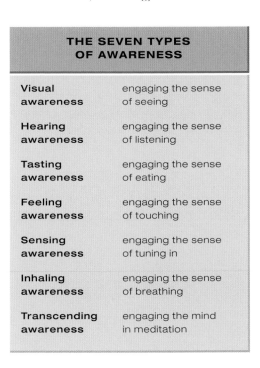

THE SEVEN TYPES OF AWARENESS	
Visual awareness	engaging the sense of seeing
Hearing awareness	engaging the sense of listening
Tasting awareness	engaging the sense of eating
Feeling awareness	engaging the sense of touching
Sensing awareness	engaging the sense of tuning in
Inhaling awareness	engaging the sense of breathing
Transcending awareness	engaging the mind in meditation

LIKE WITH LIKE ALWAYS BRINGS LUCK

One of the primary doctrines of Taoist feng shui is the concept of matching 'like with like', which uses an intuitive approach. Basically this refers to the matching of your personal chi with the chi of your immediate space and environment. How you interpret this tenet is up to you – you can take a totally simplistic approach or you can make the matching as complex as you wish. Basically, the concept of 'like with like' refers to the mind's symbolic associations. Ask yourself the following:

Do your directions match?

In the simple approach, the season of your birth determines the direction that brings you good luck. Taoists associate the east with spring, the south with summer, the west with autumn and the north with winter. So if you move from your place of birth toward your seasonal birth direction, you will have good fortune. In the complex approach, you use the directions of your

Kua formula (see pages 58–61) to tap like with like.

Do your days match?

If, for instance, you were born on the 25th of any month, then the number 25 is good for you, a house address with the number 25 in it will be lucky for you, and so forth. And if you were born on a Thursday, then every Thursday is lucky for you. This is the simplistic approach to numerology, focusing on the number we remember most easily.

Do your numbers match?

Your numbers are based on your date of birth (there is no need to change this to the lunar date since your inner chi identifies with your Western birth date). Look at your birth date expressed as numbers. If you were born on 18 March 1976, then your numbers would be 18 3 1976 – any of these numbers appearing on your address, your telephone number or your car registration would be in affinity with you.

Do your colours match?

This is based on your birth season. If you were born in the spring, your colour is green; in the summer it is red, in the winter it is black, in the autumn it is white and in between it is yellow. Wearing your colours will bring you like with like good fortune. Also, wearing red or pinks will bring you a lover or spouse, yellow will enhance your wealth luck, green will reduce stress and aggravation, and white will help you recover from an illness. This simplistic approach to feng shui is said to be as effective as using the concept of the five elements.

RIGHT Your birthday date holds the key to your personal lucky numbers. For instance, if you were born on the 11th day of the month, then the number 11 would usually be lucky for you. Like with like always brings luck.

THE CONCEPT OF DOUBLE GOODNESS

The Taoist concept of double goodness has been incorporated into the practice of feng shui. Here the reasoning is that when you have determined a number, a colour, a direction or an element that brings luck for you, then having it doubled will bring you double the luck, double the goodness, double the happiness. When you apply the concept of double goodness, think of all the good things in your life doubling in magnitude – that is, your wealth doubled, your success, and your generosity doubled as well.

Selecting double goodness days

If 8 is good for you, for example, then the 8th day of the 8th month is double goodness for you. Such a day will be doubly excellent for you to move to a new house, to start renovation, to get married or to undertake any of the happiness events in your life. Applying the double goodness concept to the selection of lucky days is one of the easiest ways of finding a day whose chi is said to be in affinity with your chi.

Selecting double goodness directions

You can also apply the double goodness principle in the practice of Eight Mansions feng shui – thus, if a certain direction is auspicious for you, then having it as your facing as well as your sitting direction will bring you a double dose of good fortune. So if north is your romance direction, your house faces north and your bedroom is located in the north sector of your house, you will enjoy double romance luck; or if southwest brings you romance luck, your room is also located in the southwest

and you sleep with your head pointing southwest, this will bring you double the romance luck you seek.

You can also apply the double goodness concept to your directions based on your birth season. Thus, if you were born in the spring, your lucky direction would be east. Then if your house faced east and you were occupying the east room, you would be enjoying double goodness luck.

ABOVE When you are moving into a new home, choose the day carefully. Either use the Almanac or apply the concept of double goodness in your selection of the days.

GOING WITH THE FLOW

Taoist teachings always stress the benefits of moving along with nature. Going with the flow means not fighting against the direction of the wind, not swimming against the currents, not attempting to turn back the clock and refraining from creating imbalances to the energy around you. Going with the flow also suggests symmetry, so that a natural balance of energy is achieved at all times. It is for this reason that feng shui recommends regular rather than irregular shapes, curves rather than angles and sharp edges, a meandering rather than a straight line. There is rhythm to the flow of life, to the changing of seasons, and to the transformation of yin into yang and back into yin again.

The simplest example of going with the flow can be experienced in how we react to the change of seasons. In winter, when it is cold, we wear heavy clothing for warmth. In summer we cool ourselves with lighter clothing.

In the materials we use to build our homes, we must ensure that the wood we use has the grain running in the same direction, that the marble on the floor flows in generally the same direction and the slate tiles we use also move in generally the same direction – all going with the flow. The flow of chi within the home should be natural so that physical flows neither meet obstacles nor are stopped abruptly.

TESTING THE WIND

Feng shui captures the essence of wind and water. You need to test the wind – see if it is excessively dry or wet, if it's gushing too fast or murmuring gently. Dry winds contain no moisture and do not bring goodness. Fast winds drive all goodness away. The winds also bring signs – messages from the cosmos. Here is how to read the wind for signs:

1 Choose the correct hour according to your animal sign (below). You can check your animal sign on pages 24–25.

Rat – 11pm to 1am
Ox – 1am to 3am
Tiger – 3am to 5am
Rabbit – 5am to 7am
Dragon – 7am to 9am
Snake – 9am to 11am
Horse – 11am to 1pm
Sheep – 1pm to 3pm
Monkey – 3pm to 5pm
Rooster – 5pm to 7pm
Dog – 7pm to 9pm
Pig – 9pm to 11pm

If the time falls in the middle of the night, use the time frame that is directly opposite

RIGHT Testing the wind requires practice. When you first try to do it, gently close your eyes and tune in to the breeze; in time you will come to develop a sensitivity and your inner consciousness will help you read the quality of the wind.

– for example, those born under the sign of the Tiger can use the hour of the Monkey to test the wind (of course, if you do not mind waking up at 3am, it would be far more accurate).

2 Test the wind from outside the main front door. Take three big steps outside, then using a compass to determine your orientation, turn to face south. Next relax all your body sensors. Focus in on the seven types of awareness and open yourself to the wind that is blowing at that precise moment. Remember to stay quite relaxed at all times. If there is a gentle breeze, the signs are excellent. If the wind is gushing and strong, good luck is swept away. The more windy it is, the more protection the house needs. If there is no wind at all, the energy is stuck and the house needs its energy woken up. You can use sounds or music or throw a party to bring in an infusion of yang energy.

3 If you are testing the winds for romance luck, look for signs related to the earth element. Look for things in pairs, such as birds, bees and butterflies. Look out for things passing by that are red or yellow in colour. Look for the moon, for women, smiling faces, flowers blooming. Anything at all in nature can be read as answers to the questions in your mind at that moment you decide to test the wind. If you are doing this investigation for a friend, use the hour that corresponds to his or her animal sign.

4 If you are testing the wind for wealth luck, look for signs related to both wind and water, either combined or singly. The most potent signal for wealth and prosperity is rain. A light rain is excellent. You only have to beware of hurricanes and storms. Everything else is excellent. Thunder and lightning are claps of approval. Also check clouds – the presence of light white clouds is always a good sign. Look at the cars and vans that drive past. When something suggests money or a harvest, or a fully loaded lorry drives by, these are instantly good signs. Sailing ships, a busload of children, a neighbour's cat jumping by are all good signs.

ABOVE Lightning often brings some messages to those who are able to read signs from nature. When the sky is suddenly brightened by lightning when you are looking for a sign, it usually suggests a major opportunity is coming your way.

171

SENSING THE CHI

Chi is really the wind, just as money is water. Chi brings all the attributes of happiness and brings out the power inherent in water, which brings wealth. So while water is vital and important, chi is even more so. When you test the wind you are in reality sensing the chi around you. Below you will find the important signs to look out for.

BELOW To get the best feng shui luck from flowers, choose the colours carefully. Yellow flowers usually suggest money luck while pink flowers indicate good fortune associated with love.

Health luck

When testing the wind for health luck, look for signs of movement that reveal the presence of yang chi, such as a gentle breeze; or the colour white, which always means healing and a renewal; or the sun

suddenly appearing from behind clouds. This is such a powerful symbol of yang energy that recovery is certain. Each time you suddenly become aware of the sun shining through trees, or coming out from behind clouds, it is always a sign of recovery.

Business luck

When sensing the chi for clues to business luck, look for signs related to the wood element. If you see a lorry carrying a load of logs, or transporting furniture, these are excellent signs. Flowers, plants, a view of water, or suddenly turning on the TV and finding there is a picture of a forest of trees or a field of flowers blooming – these are excellent signs that your business is going to succeed. Recently I was looking at a friend's house feng shui. She is starting a new business venture and wanted to ensure her feng shui was auspicious. At the precise moment I started looking for signs, I looked up to the clouds above her house and spied truly auspicious cloud formations that took the shape of dragons. This was indeed a good sign. According to Taoist feng shui, this indicates that her luck is good and her business will succeed.

Money luck

To sense the chi for sudden money luck, look for signs of prosperity, such as the appearance of coins, or suddenly seeing an image of a river – on television as you switch it on, or on the page you turn to in a magazine, or rain suddenly falling, or a bird flying towards you. Birds, generally speaking, are the best indicators of sudden

wealth. When you hang pictures of birds or paintings of many birds, it suggests great good fortune coming towards you. Paintings of cranes (symbols of longevity) are also said to bring sudden money luck when they are painted as a flock and flying in the skies.

Signs from flowers

When a plant that rarely flowers suddenly blooms, it is also a very good sign. Flowers also indicate extreme good fortune when you are looking for signs that indicate how a business venture will turn out. Flowers blossoming suggest a project coming to a successful fruition. Yellow flowers indicate money success, while white flowers can suggest a bad situation getting better. White blooms also suggest someone who is sick getting well. Pink flowers suggest good fortune associated with romantic luck – they are a much better indication than red flowers. Indeed, sending red roses to someone you love is usually frowned upon by those who practise feng shui, since red roses can cause relationships to end. This is especially true of roses that have thorns – it is always better to send pink or peach roses with the thorns removed. The indications of auspicious colours for flowers should be observed when displaying flowers for the home. Let these be one of the first things you see in the morning as you eat breakfast and one of the last things that you see at night. This creates powerful vibes within your mind.

ABOVE Sunlight peeping through the trees suggests the good fortune chi associated with bright yang energy. This picture shows yang energy brightening up a forest of bare trees. To dream of a sunrise in this context is a good omen.

SIGNS FROM CHILDREN

ABOVE Young children are acutely sensitive to chi, especially young boys below the age of nine. Watching them will give you an idea of the quality of the surrounding chi.

Young children personify 'pure yang' chi. Their behaviour, their responses and the way they are dressed are signs that tell you about the quality of energy in any space. Boys under nine years old are said to reflect the good and bad side of energy that dominates any home. Young boys are also used by Nature to communicate with us, so be alert to their behaviour if they should suddenly appear at the exact hour you are testing the wind and sensing the chi. Observe what children do. If they are playing, watch the games they play. Are the games stable or unstable? Are they happily reading? Are they building something? Does it suggest anything related to what you are doing? For instance, if you were in business, then anything they do that is related to building, growing or eating would be good signs. If they offer you anything – sweets, coins or paper – these too are excellent signs.

Also watch their moods. Are they happy, smiling and laughing? Are they unhappy or restless? A happy child always suggests good feng shui, while an unhappy, fretful display of anger or tears suggests that there might be pockets of negative energy and that some space cleansing is required before a feng shui alteration can be made. When the child demands to go home, it is almost certain that there is something negative in the energy.

Look at the clothes they are wearing. Are they too tight or too loose? Do they look comfortable? Are the colours in harmony with your home? Children wearing white, green, yellow, red or bright blue bring the yang vibrations of the four directions. Children coming into your home wearing black signifies yang confined in yin and is a very bad sign indeed.

Look at photos or paintings of children in the home. There are few things as auspicious as young children grinning broadly and looking happy. Pictures like this exude pure yang energy that is favourable, while pictures that suggest children are in discomfort, pain or grief are to be avoided.

SIGNS FROM BIRDS

How many birds do you see?

- A single black bird indicates an important message.
- A pair of birds means love is coming your way.
- A family of birds suggests the possibility of a new addition to the family or a family reunion, which brings happiness.

Do you see healthy or injured birds?

- An injured bird is a warning. Be careful for the rest of the day. Drive slowly.
- A healthy lively bird suggests a happy occasion.
- Several birds chirping merrily means increased social partying.
- When birds are singing, it is a happy sign suggesting a busier social life.

What colour birds do you see?

- A white bird means healing. If someone close to you is desperately ill, this is a sign of recovery.
- A bird with red markings means an honour of some kind is coming to you.
- A yellow bird means sudden wealth or a happiness occasion (such as a pregnancy).
- A blue bird means promotion at work.

What kind of birds do you see?

- Magpies mean new friends coming into your life.
- Birds of prey always mean wealth; the eagle, for instance, suggests good fortune.
- Small birds, such as sparrows, indicate good news – these are happy messengers.
- Lovebirds suggest romance or meeting a soulmate.
- Crows mean some divine message can be expected – perhaps having a prophetic dream.
- Owls indicate a teacher of great significance coming into your life.

In feng shui, birds are powerful symbols of new opportunity and so the Crimson Phoenix – the celestial queen of all feathered creatures – is the ultimate symbol of new opportunities during times of adversity. Having the Phoenix image in the home is said to attract prosperity and abundance. A hundred phoenixes would be a hundred times more auspicious.

Other birds, even bird feathers, are also regarded with favour. Birds signify protection for those who take financial and business risks. When placed in the South, birds ward off bad business luck. Roosters deflect gossip and politicking. Birds of prey bring wealth, and bird feathers protect from accidents during travel. Hanging even a toy bird with real bird feathers at the back of a car is powerful protection from accidents. In Taoist feng shui, birds are regarded as cosmic messengers.

Birds flying towards you are the best signals. Birds flying away from you suggest a missed opportunity. A bird flying upwards is a good sign. Birds singing in the morning bring good news. When birds build nests in your garden, it is a very good sign heralding prosperity or increased income.

ABOVE Birds almost always signify good fortune and the more birds you can capture in any image or painting the luckier it is. Birds are said to be the messengers of the Immortals, and birds in your home spell good fortune. Even bird feathers are said to possess protective attributes.

STRENGTHENING THE EARTH CHI

An easy Taoist feng shui way to enhance the quality of energy in your home is to strengthen its earth chi. Earth chi is so important that in the old days this was almost synonymous with good feng shui.

ABOVE This classical Chinese landscape painting signifies the strengthening of earth chi. A popular subject, it is hung in many homes to attract good feng shui.

Taoist feng shui accepts that heaven and earth combined establishes the natural phenomena upon which man builds. This is the trinity of tien, ti, ren – or heaven, earth and mankind. In this trinity, earth chi has the most significant influence on your fortunes. Here are six ways to strengthen it in and around your home:

▨ Always have earth materials as your ground floor. Use marble, granite or tiles. Solid slabs of tiles or marble are better than broken marble or terrazzo. Anything broken or in a haphazard design suggests an unstable foundation. Avoid having wood or carpets on your ground floor.

▨ Surround your home with rocks to bring good vibrations – a few rocks placed at the four corners suggests the earth chi is strong and stable. You can also build a symbolic mountain of gold (a pile of rocks with some gold leaf stuck to them) to create a direct connection with the earth/heaven axis. This is very auspicious.

▨ Create a wall behind the home to signify the mountain giving you support. This need not be a massive wall – anything 1.2m (4ft) and above is sufficient. A wall is always better than trees to give you support.

▨ Create a square patch filled with sand or pebbles to strengthen the earth chi of the front of the house. This strengthens the symbolism of earth element energy.

▨ Manifest the three powerful earth numbers of 2, 5 and 8. You could use, for example, two round crystals, five yellow rocks and eight medium-sized pebbles. You can stress whichever number you wish. Since Period Eight is coming (see pages 84–85), emphasizing eight will bring good fortune. The numbers 2, 5, and 8 are described as parent string numbers in the Flying Star system of feng shui and when they occur together, they manifest great good fortune.

▨ Hang a painting of a strong and solid-looking mountain in the home to support your endeavours. In Flying Star feng shui, a mountain image in the corner of the home or living room that houses the mountain star 8 brings enormous good fortune in health and relationships. The mountain painting is also incredibly lucky when hung behind you at work or, indeed, wherever you are sitting. This is a symbol of powerful earth chi and is required for upward career mobility as well as the preservation of one's wealth.

MYSTICAL MUDRAS TO DETECT CHI

You can use mystical hand signals (called mudras) to check the chi of your home. Sometimes the chi works in such mysterious ways that the reason for a family problem could be hidden. If things suddenly start going wrong and you feel there might be something wrong with your feng shui, but you are unable to find the cause, then try using these mystical mudras.

Always start with the protection mudra (top right). Hold both your hands out in front of you in the protection mudra. First close your fingers into a fist and then straighten the index and little fingers. Hold your hands with palms facing upward in this position and slowly walk round the rooms of the house. At first you will feel nothing, but after a while you will start to get a small tingling sensation in your hands. This protection mudra ensures that you do not 'collide' with negative energy as you walk around the room. Remember to keep your spine straight and erect as this will ensure chi flows through your body unimpeded, thereby facilitating your investigation.

Feeling for difficult energy

To investigate and uncover negative energy that may be causing you harm but is not obvious, use the investigation mudra (bottom right).

To do this, bring the two hands together in the previous position and join the fingers of both hands, index finger to index finger, little finger to little finger, and thumb to thumb. With the two hands joined in this way you can walk around the rooms of the home a second time. Your hands will help you to resolve and detect difficult chi energy. When the energy is negative you will feel a tingling in your hands. Often closer inspection will reveal the cause of any illness or problem area, such as damage to a symbolic feng shui enhancer.

LEFT Shown here are two very powerful hand signals known as mudras. If you use these mudras to investigate the feng shui of a home they can reveal hidden problems. But mudras are best practised under the tutelage of a master.

ABOVE This powerful feng shui symbol, the mystical knot, is made from coins tied together. This is so powerful that it can transform bad energy into good energy.

RIGHT The Chinese have always valued semi-precious stones such as yellow amber. Believed to be a sacred gemstone, it can be worn as a protective amulet.

USING MYSTICAL SYMBOLS

There are so many different symbols, an entire book could be written about them. But the three most widely used are longevity symbols such as the God of Longevity, the mystical endless knot and the 'ru yi', the symbol for power and authority. These can be made from different materials but they are imbued with extra power when carved from crystals and semi-precious stones. To be able to empower these symbols with added vitality would usually require direct initiation from a qualified Taoist Master.

Taoist feng shui has many versions of mystic symbols, which can be empowered to become talismans and amulets. In the past the patriarchs and ladies of the upper classes wore these mystic symbols. The mandarins and officials at court also wore them as part of their official attire. These symbols were often worn either as rings or as pins. Some were worn as hairpieces and others were worn hidden inside robes and secret belts.

Protective amulets were often drawn with sacred prayers written in fancy calligraphy and then consecrated by monks or other holy men. Special auspicious and sacred gemstones such as blue lapis lazuli, red coral, turquoise, yellow amber, green jade and pearl-coloured moonstones were also incorporated as finely embedded decorative energy enhancers. The selection of stones was usually based on astrological calculations. Whenever coloured stones were used, these would be fairly large pieces as they often doubled as symbols of authority, as well as representing the five elements.

Popular talismanic jewellery worn by the senior court members and army generals included symbols such as the ru yi, the longevity symbol and the mystical knot (this is such a powerful sign that merely drawing the symbol in the air with your hands will transform bad energy into good energy). These three symbols had significant meanings and when empowered were believed to bring better health, strength and vigour, while protecting the wearer from unnatural death, such as by accident or execution. Mystical symbols and powerful gemstones transcend the passage of time and are as potent in today's world as they were in past eras.

178

SYMBOLS TO PROTECT FROM EXCESSIVE YIN CHI

Yin forces can be harmful to the energy of yang spaces, and this manifests in different ways. At home, sickness and quarrels can be the result of strong yin forces. At work, yin chi can cause severe stress and back-stabbing. The result is the pernicious presence of hidden enemies. Friends can become adversaries under such conditions. This kind of work environment is very stressful indeed.

Yin forces should be kept at a minimum and never be allowed to dominate any space. In feng shui, this affliction is referred to as yin spirit formation, which, at its least harmful, causes inconvenient illnesses and small accidents, but at its worst can cause severe illness. Yin forces also cause backache, arthritis and sciatica pains and older people are much more susceptible to yin chi attacks. Thus yin spirit formation should always be chased away, or transformed into yang energy. Give your home a yang energy bath by frequently opening the windows and doors to receive new flows of energy. Playing music, holding dinner parties and having young people in the home all raise precious yang energy.

Dealing with office politics

When yin forces get too strong and seem to be hitting the more vulnerable members of the family or workforce, you might need specific cures. Many people suffer from this problem at work, and are unhappy simply because someone at the office is gossiping and putting them down. In Taoist feng shui, the rooster image is the most popular cure, as it symbolically gobbles up all negative gossip. A porcelain rooster painted in gold is powerful. So are rooster images painted in white or in red and gold, because fire and metal energy will overcome any quarrelsome and sickness energy.

Red and gold Happiness Buddha images are equally excellent cures for Flying Star afflictions caused by the quarrelsome star 3, and especially the combinations 3/2 and 2/3. A completely golden Laughing Buddha is also suitable, but a touch of red strengthens the remedy. Let the Buddha sit facing the direction of anyone you suspect is causing you trouble – this transforms potential grief into actual happiness.

Coin swords and the placement of support symbols behind your desk can supplement roosters very effectively. These should be placed on the wall on the left side of the facing direction of your desk. Hang a coin sword with its hilt up and its blade side pointing down – the symbolism is a powerful remedy when used with respect and diligence.

The most powerful of the support symbols are the military Gods such as Kuan Kung, the dragon tortoise and of course mountains, which can be symbolized by suitable mountain paintings.

LEFT There are few symbols that have as many protective connotations as the mystical tortoise. The tortoise shown here is carved out of white marble. Placing something like this in the home is excellent feng shui.

THE SIGNIFICANCE OF TREES

Taoists regard healthy, well-cared for trees as a major source of growth chi and believe that those who live in homes devoid of trees will lack the impetus for growth.

Taoist feng shui considers the presence of trees around the home as an essential component of good feng shui, although there are simple guidelines to be followed:

■ Broadleaved trees are preferred to thin, spiky-leaved trees. Bamboo and pines are exceptions, as these are regarded as powerful symbols of longevity; but bamboo should always be planted in the front of the house for it to bring good fortune.

■ A single tree in a central open courtyard means 'difficulty' and should be avoided.

■ Five trees behind the house simulate the mountain support. Fruit trees symbolize that the support is also nurturing. The trees should look healthy and strong.

■ A dead tree behind the house is bad luck, and a dead tree in front is even worse, so do remove these. Old people are especially susceptible to dead-tree energy.

■ Trees and plants on the left side of the home will control the husband's anger and benefit him, while plants on the right side will control the wife's anger and benefit her, so it is a good idea to plant on both sides.

BELOW Trees that have good foliage and whose leaves are rounded and broad are preferable to trees that have thin, spiky leaves.

AUSPICIOUS TREES

■ Red date trees and pomegranate plants are said to bring pregnancy and recovery luck.

■ Lime trees dispel bad energy that hurts the household.

■ Apple trees bring peace and harmony to the home.

■ Orange trees bring wealth and prosperity.

■ Willow trees bring tears and hard work.

ACTIVATING WEALTH CHI WITH COINS

A popular method of activating wealth luck when building a new home is to lace the floor and walls with coins tied with red ribbons. This creates good earth energy that attracts good luck.

Taoist feng shui recommends the lavish use of coins to activate wealth luck for the home. When a house is being built or renovated, place coins activated with red string or ribbon under the floor before the tiles are laid, and on the walls before the plaster is applied. Place the coins from the outside moving inward, all along the staircase and into the master bedroom. This will symbolize wealth coming into the home.

The ideal is to tie three coins with red or yellow string to signify yang energy. Three signifies the unity of heaven, earth and man and is thus an excellent number. Place the activated coins in the four corners of every room of the home or office. Tying the coins with a mystic knot gives them added potency and will set up wealth vibrations through the foundations. Then place three coin clusters all along the floor and walls of the living and dining rooms.

When you place the coins make sure that they are placed flat on the floors and walls. If you are using authentic coins from Imperial China, place with the yang side up. This is the side with four characters. You can be as extravagant and as greedy as you wish! You can also bury coins outside the house in the four corners of your land or property – this will signify accumulated wealth rather than mere income and suggests long-term good fortune – the ultimate goal of feng shui.

DOTTING THE EYE OF THE DRAGON

Taoist feng shui considers that there is vital energy in every celestial creature, and when these creatures have their spirit awakened by dotting their eyes, they become even more powerful.

The ritual of 'dotting the eye of the dragon' involves the symbolic awakening of this celestial creature to enhance its power. It can be undertaken in a simple ceremony using dragon paintings and dragon images placed inside homes and offices. When the dragon images in your home are energized in this way, they bring prosperity, protection and happy occasions such as births and marriages.

To dot the eye of the dragon, all you need is a black brush and black Chinese ink. The ritual can be as simple or elaborate as you wish, but it must be accompanied by an infusion of yang energy. This can be represented by the loud clashing of cymbals and drums or by having bright lights shining at the dragon. It is advisable to dot the eyes of the dragon during the dragon hour in the early morning, between 7am and 9am.

RIGHT Dragons placed near water or near an image of water are said to activate 'lucky outcomes' luck for those living in its vicinity.

THE POWER OF SMOOTH CRYSTAL BALLS

Taoist feng shui almost always stresses the vital beauty and auspiciousness of smooth and circular objects that are fashioned from crystals. Placed in the home they denote a smooth life in which projects move along with few obstacles and blockages. The best rooms to activate this way are the family, dining and living areas.

Taoist feng shui also acknowledges the efficacy of round smooth crystal balls, especially when they are made from natural rock crystals. Displayed in clusters of six or nine in the living or family areas of the home, crystal balls create energy that fosters loving relationships and ensures a smooth ride through life for residents. Quarrels are kept to a minimum and in fact soon become a thing of the past. Projects will succeed and victory is often within reach.

Crystals signify the nurturing energy of mother earth, so they also benefit the household matriarch. Placed in the southwest corners of the home, they bring wonderful family and romance luck. To activate the power of the crystals even more, try shining a bright light at them. Remember that in the southwest location, crystals bring love and a steady relationship. This will be very smooth and pleasurable if you place six crystal balls here.

Crystal balls carved with the map of the world are excellent for study and examination luck, especially when placed in the northeast of any room. In this case, one crystal ball is usually sufficient unless your child requires constant stimulation.

The choice of the type of crystal is often a personal matter. You can select whatever stone catches your fancy, though natural clear crystals are best. Yellow citrine globes and globes made of calcites are said to be excellent wealth energizers. Indeed any yellow stone strongly suggests the power of earth chi.

BELOW Place egg-shaped or rounded crystals in the home to attract a hassle-free life. Though you can choose the type you like, traditionally-oriented Taoists prefer the perfectly round shape.

POWERFUL RITUALS WITH CRYSTALS

To create good chi in your home try using any one of the three rituals described here. They are not difficult to practise but it is vital to perform these rituals with a good heart.

An amethyst gem tree is a popular symbol to bring relationship harmony to the home. It has clear crystals placed on a 'tree', which stands on an amethyst crystal. If you buy one of these make sure the amethyst has a firm base, since this strengthens all your relationships.

Below you will find three Taoist feng shui rituals that use crystals to enhance the energy of your home.

■ Bury three crystals in a triangular pattern (known as a mountain peak crystal formation) in the ground in front of your home. Make sure the peak of the triangle is pointing outward. You can use either crystal balls or a single pointed crystal.

This is a very powerful secret way of preventing bad energy from entering the home.

■ Place seven pieces of single-pointed crystal under the bed in an arrow formation with the peak pointing toward the head of the bed. Have one central crystal to form the arrow and three crystals on either side to form the head.

■ Six crystals on your work desk attracts recognition for your work. Place six crystals on the top right-hand corner of your desk to improve your concentration and creativity. If you write powerful mantras on your crystals, they bring great good fortune in all aspects of your work.

THE POWER OF AMETHYST CLUSTERS

The amethyst is regarded with great favour in Taoist feng shui practice. It is especially useful for fortifying the bonds of marriage and when placed under the bed directly under the feet of the sleeping couple it symbolically 'ties them to each other'.

Amethyst geodes with deep 'pockets' are also said to be extremely powerful in attracting wealth energy. If you want to activate the power of crystals in your home or office, you can use the amethyst or the quartz crystal. In either case, always look for thick formations of crystal. Geodes that have thin crystal formations indicate poverty vibrations and are simply of no use. Inside, the crystals formed should be deep purple in colour, since this indicates wealth. Amethysts also have the power to transform negative energy into positive energy, and yin vibrations into yang vibrations.

DISPLAYING ANIMAL SYMBOLS

Dragons, horses, lions and tortoises are all potent feng shui symbols. The tips below offer some extra advice to help you get the most from them in the home.

DRAGONS bring prosperity and success, but they are most potent when placed near water – a water feature or an aquarium. A golden dragon image carrying a pearl is best. Place one, two, five, six or nine dragons – these numbers activate the dragon image. Never place dragons near fire, in the kitchen, in the bedroom or on the floor. Also, do not keep your dragon image imprisoned in a glass case. Dragons should be free to fly upward.

Wear the dragon image as a brooch pin to ward off bad energy and protect you from being cheated or conned. Wear it as a locket to activate your heart chakra, which enhances your powers of persuasion. The best dragon images are those made of real gold and decorated with precious gemstones or diamonds.

HORSES bring recognition and fame. Tribute horses in white, led in by the God of Wealth, bring prosperity. A single black horse is the victory horse. Horses running in panic bring extreme fear and misfortunes. Workhorses suggest work without recognition and should never be displayed in the home.

Horses are best displayed either singly or in groups of eight. They should never be displayed in fives or fours – indeed four horses suggest a terrible accident or death.

LIONS can be quite dangerous for your neighbours, so it is better to use Chi Lins or Fu dogs (see page 27). When using lions for protection, they should be placed on the ground and never high up on gateposts.

TORTOISES bring loads of good energy. You can keep any number, but a single tortoise is usually the best form of protection. They are best placed at the back of the home or in the North part of the garden. Golden tortoises with dragon heads are even more potent as protector images.

BELOW The wealth god Tsai Shen Yeh leading the tribute horse into your home is a particularly powerful symbol of wealth. Note the horse is laden with gold ingots.

GLOSSARY

Auspicious feng shui This means enjoying the eight types of feng shui luck. These are wealth, good health, a good family life, a long life, good luck with children, good mentors, a good reputation and a good education.

Bad feng shui This is the opposite of the above. Most bad feng shui can be ameliorated with the appropriate cures.

Chen This trigram's element is big wood, its direction is east and it governs our roots and ancestors and the spirit of the first male descendant.

Chi An intangible force in everyone and everything. It can be positive as in Sheng Chi (growth breath) or negative as in Shar Chi (killing breath).

Chi kung A form of exercise that enables practitioners to move the chi around them.

Chien This trigram's element is big metal, its direction is northwest and it signifies helpful mentors and the patriarch and leader.

Destructive cycle The cycle of elements in which wood devours earth, which destroys water, which kills fire, which consumes metal, which destroys wood. This cycle must be followed to ensure that the elements of objects, directions and locations in any room do not destroy one another.

Fuk Luk Sau Three feng shui gods, respectively, the God of Wealth and Happiness, the God of High Rank and Affluence, and the God of Health and Longevity.

Kan This trigram's element is water, its direction is north and it governs career and represents the second son of the family.

Ken This trigram's element is small earth, its direction is northeast, it signifies education and represents the second son of the family.

Kua numbers Part of the Eight Mansions formula. They are derived from a person's year of birth and sex and are the key to determining a person's auspicious or inauspicious directions.

Kun This trigram's element is big earth, its direction is southwest, it signifies relationships and represents the matriarch and mother.

Li This trigram's element is fire, its direction is south, it governs reputation and represents the second daughter of the family.

Lo Shu square The three by three grid with nine numbers on which feng shui compass formulas are based.

Pa Kua An eight-sided symbol that has trigrams arranged around the eight sides. Each trigram gives meaning to the eight major directions of the compass, which are also shown on the Pa Kua. South is always shown at the top.

Poison arrow A straight or sharp structure, from which chi bounces off at an angle, creating harmful energy.

Productive cycle The cycle of elements in which water feeds wood, which feeds fire, which makes earth, which in turn holds water. This cycle must be taken into account to ensure that the elements of objects, directions and locations in any room do not destroy one another.

Sun This trigram's element is small wood, its direction is southeast, it governs wealth and prosperity and represents the eldest daughter of the family.

Trigram A symbol made of broken or unbroken lines symbolizing the way in which yin and yang combine to make chi. There are eight trigrams, and each has a different combination of broken and unbroken lines and carries different associations.

Tui This trigram's element is small metal, its direction is west, it governs creativity and children and represents the youngest daughter of the family.

Yang Creative energy, thought of as active and masculine.

Yin Receptive energy, thought of as passive and feminine.

FURTHER INFORMATION

Lillian Too's author website:
www.lillian-too.com
Lillian Too's Internet feng shui magazine:
www.wofs.com
Lillian Too's feng shui Ecommerce:
www.fsmegamall.com
Lillian Too's email:
ltoo@wofs.com

Other books by Lillian Too:
Basic Feng Shui
Easy to Use Feng Shui – 168 Ways to Health, Wealth and Happiness
Eight Mansions Feng Shui

Feng Shui for the Gardener
Feng Shui Magic
Feng Shui Success Secrets
Feng Shui Symbols of Good Fortune
Flying Star Feng Shui for the Master Practitioner
168 Feng Shui Ways to Declutter Your Home
Period 8 Feng Shui
Personalized Feng Shui Tips
Practical Applications of Feng Shui
Smart Feng Shui for the Home
The Complete Feng Shui Reference Book
The Complete Illustrated Guide to Feng Shui
The Feng Shui Encyclopaedia
Water Feng Shui for Wealth

INDEX

ACKNOWLEDGEMENTS

Picture Credits

Corbis: pp. 10 Brownie Harris, 13 Elizabeth Whiting & Associates, 20 Michael Nicholson, 22bl Roger Tidman, 39 Elizabeth Whiting & Associates, 47 Owen Franken, 48 Gareth Brown, 49 Massimo Listri, 53 Peter Harholdt, 55 Chris Collins, 64 SIE Productions, 82 Gen Pau, 91 Michael Freeman, 113 Mark L Stephenson, 122 Chris Hellier, 123 Di Lewis/Elizabeth Whiting & Associates, 125 Elizabeth Whiting & Associates, 126, 133 Michael Boys, 134 Christies Images, 136t Alexander Burkatowski, 136m Edimedia, 137 National Gallery Collection; By kind Permission of the Trustees of the National Gallery, London, 142 Austrian Archives/ Osterreichische Galerie Vienna, 144 Keren Su, 146 Elizabeth Whiting & Associates, 151 Rodney Hyett/ Elizabeth Whiting & Associates, 158 Scott Faulkner, 163 Gina Sabatella, 169 David Brooks, 174 Paul Barton, 182 Leonard de Selva

Getty Images: pp. 7 Taxi/Rob Melnychuk, 29 Stone/Timothy Shonnard, 42 Stone/Paul Redman, 115 Taxi/Stephen Simpson, 120, 127 Taxi/Kit Latham, 154 Taxi/Peter Gridley, 155 Taxi/David Sacks, 171 Image Bank/A.T.Willett, 172 Taxi/Jeremy Samuelson, 180 Image Bank/John and | Lisa Merrill

Thanks also go to Wofs.com for permission to use their pictures on the following pages: pp. 5, 6, 8, 50, 95tr, 140, 141, 185

Author's Credits

This book is dedicated with love to my wonderful students all over the world who are doing great work popularising the wonderful living skill of feng shui, and especially to my family – Jennifer, Wan Jin, Chris, Phillip, Honey, and Han Jin; to my young team of super creative people – Cheryl, Connie, Nickque, Kenji, Sky, Mavis, Liong, Stanley, Janice, Gopal, Loke and also to Peter and Jason. What would my life be without all of you? Thank you for bringing me so much happiness and fulfillment.

Publisher's Acknowledgements

Executive Editor: David Alexander
Managing Editor: Clare Churly
Production Manager: Louise Hall

Designed and produced for Hamlyn by The Bridgewater Book Company

Creative Director: Terry Jeavons
Editorial Director: Jason Hook
Project designer: Lisa McCormick
Page make-up: Alistair Plumb
Editors: Jenni Davis, Susie Behar
Illustrators: Richard Constable and Sarah Young
Photographer: Mike Helmsley
Picture Researcher: Vanessa Fletcher

Special thanks go to
Tizz's, Lewes
Oriental Arts, Brighton
David and Alison Payne